CHRIST IS THE ANSWER

CHRIST IS THE ANSWER

The Christ-Centered Teaching of Pope John Paul II

John Saward

ALBA·HOUSE   NEW·YORK

SOCIETY OF ST. PAUL, 2187 VICTORY BLVD., STATEN ISLAND, NEW YORK 10314

Published in Great Britain by T&T Clark Ltd,
59 George Street, Edinburgh EH2 2LQ, Scotland

This edition published under license from T&T Clark Ltd by
Alba House, Society of St Paul,
2187 Victory Boulevard, Staten Island, New York 10314

First published 1995

Library of Congress Cataloging-in-Publication Data

Saward John.
    Christ is the answer: the Christ-centered teaching of Pope John
Paul II/John Saward.
        p.   cm.
    Includes bibliographical references.
    ISBN 0-8189-0746-0
        1. John Paul II. Pope, 1920– . 2. Catholic Church—Doctrines—
History—20th century.   3. Jesus Christ—History of doctrines—20th
century.   I. Title.
    BX1378.5.S2B   1995
    230'.2'082—de20   95-19053
                                                        CIP

Published by Alba House, the publishing division of the Fathers and Brothers of the Society of St. Paul,
2187 Victory Boulevard, Staten Island, New York 10314,
as part of their communications apostolate.

Printing Information:

Current Printing - first digit	2	3	4	5	6	7	8	9	10

Year of Current Printing - first year shown

	1996		1997		1998		1999		2000

Nihil obstat: Joseph F. Martino (*Censor Librorum*)
Imprimatur: Anthony J. Bevilacqua (*Archiepiscopus Philadelphiensis*)
6 April 1995

Typeset by Waverley Typesetters, Galashiels
Printed and bound in Great Britain by Page Bros, Norwich

Contents

Acknowledgements   vii

Abbreviations   ix

Introduction   xi

Part I   Christ the Centre

1   The Meaning of 'Christocentricity'   1
2   Pope John Paul's Christocentricity   11

Part II   The Whole Christ

3   'You are Christ': The Confession of Peter   17
4   One of the Trinity   21
5   The Christocentric Mary   27
6   The Saviour   45
7   Cosmos in Christ   55
8   The Church of Christ   63
9   The Eucharistic Christ   69

Part III   Christ the Answer

10   Man Revealed in Christ   75
11   Life in Christ   91
12   The Mission of Christ the Redeemer   101
13   The Christ-Centred Priest   113

Conclusion   133

Index   135

Acknowledgements

This book started life as a paper presented to a conference organized in Washington DC by *Communio* under the chairmanship of Professor David L. Schindler. I should like to thank David for the invitation to speak on that occasion and for the enjoyable years I worked with him on the board of *Communio*. The chapter on 'The Christ-Centred Priest' is based on talks I gave to the priests of the Archdiocese of Philadelphia. I want also to express my gratitude to the Rector of St Charles Borromeo Seminary, Monsignor Daniel A. Murray, for his unfailingly generous support of my work as a teacher and writer. I hope that he enjoys this book on John Paul II. Throughout his Rectorship, he has striven to maintain and strengthen St Charles' tradition of loyalty to the Holy Father. He has built up an atmosphere of Christian friendship and Catholic orthodoxy in which it is a joy to live and work. Among my other friends and colleagues at St Charles, I must thank especially Monsignor Richard Malone, Dr Atherton Lowry, and Dr John Thornbrugh for many valuable insights into the thought of Karol Wojtyla.

This book belongs above all to my wife, Christine, and my youngest daughter, Anna, who have shared the American adventure with me over the last two years, including the hectic weeks when I was attempting to complete the manuscript of this book and was therefore more than usually distracted. Most of the text was put on to disc by Christine, and for that I am sincerely grateful. But the book is hers in a much deeper sense. Fifteen years ago, during the first year of the pontificate of Pope

John Paul II, Christine came with me into the Catholic Church, leaving behind a beautiful Cornish rectory and all the other comforts of Anglican clerical life. For sharing the Catholic adventure with me, I dedicate this book to her.

JOHN SAWARD
St Charles Borromeo Seminary, Wynnewood, Pennsylvania

13 May 1994
Feast of Our Lady of Fatima

Abbreviations

AAS	*Acta Apostolicae Sedis*
CA	*Centesimus Annus* (Pope John Paul II)
Catechesi	*Catechesi del mercoledì* (Casale Monferrato, 1988) (Pope John Paul II)
CCC	*The Catechism of the Catholic Church*
CCSL	*Corpus Christianorum: Series Latina*
CL	*Christifideles Laici* (Pope John Paul II)
Decreta	*Vaticanum II: Constitutiones, Decreta, Declarationes* (Vatican City, 1966)
DM	*Dives in Misericordia* (Pope John Paul II)
DVb	*Dei Verbum* (Vatican II)
DV	*Dominum et Vivificantem* (Pope John Paul II)
DS	Denzinger-Schönmetzer, *Enchiridion Symbolorum*
ET	English Translation
FC	*Familiaris Consortio* (Pope John Paul II)
GS	*Gaudium et Spes* (Vatican II)
LG	*Lumen Gentium* (Vatican II)
Maria	*Maria – Gottes Ja zum Menschen*. Enzyklika 'Mutter des Erlösers' (Freiburg, 1987) (Pope John Paul II)
MD	*Mulieris Dignitatem* (Vatican II)
OT	*Optatam Totius* (Vatican II)
PDV	*Pastores Dabo Vobis* (Pope John Paul II)
PG	*Patrologia Graeca*
PL	*Patrologia Latina*
PO	*Presbyterorum Ordinis* (Vatican II)
RH	*Redemptor Hominis* (Pope John Paul II)

RM   *Redemptoris Mater* (Pope John Paul II)
Rmi   *Redemptoris Missio* (Pope John Paul II)
SC   *Sources Chrétiennes*
SD   *Salvifici Doloris* (Pope John Paul II)
ST   *Summa Theologiae* (St Thomas Aquinas)
TD   *Theodramatik* (Hans Urs von Balthasar)
VS   *Veritatis Splendor* (Pope John Paul II)

The dates given in the footnotes refer to addresses and homilies of the Pope. The text can be found in the relevant volume of the collected *Insegnamenti* of Pope John Paul II.

Introduction

The Christ-Centred Pope

In Rome, in the church of St Paul-Outside-the-Walls, there is a dazzling icon of a Christ-centred Pope. It is the mosaic in the apse, commissioned by Honorius III and executed by three Venetian masters. The towering middle figure is the risen Jesus, His right hand raised in blessing, His left opening the Gospels at the words, 'Come, O blessed of my Father' (cf. Matt. 25.34). He is flanked by four lesser giants – St Peter with St Andrew, St Paul with St Luke. At the Pantocrator's feet is a tiny, crumpled figure. From a distance it looks like a white rabbit, but closer inspection reveals it to be Pope Honorius himself, prostrate in worship, overwhelmed by the glory of God shining in the face of Jesus Christ. 'He is all', Honorius seems to be saying, 'I am nothing.'

Cardinal de Lubac saw this mosaic as a symbol of the pontificate of Paul VI. Like Honorius, Pope Paul 'wanted to be literally crushed to the ground, to be tiny in the presence of a great Christ upright in majesty'.[1] His mission was 'to testify that the Church is nothing if she is not the handmaid of Christ, if she does not reflect His light, if she does not transmit His life'.[2] Paul was convinced that only an attitude of Christ-centredness could open up the teaching of the Second Vatican Council:

[1] H. de Lubac, *Entretien autour de Vatican II. Souvenirs et réflexions* (Paris, 1985), p. 25.
[2] Ibid.

If we want to understand the central doctrine of the Council, we must understand the Church, but to understand the Church we must refer everything to Christ.[3]

The fire of Christocentricity which burnt so brightly in Paul VI now blazes with extraordinary intensity in John Paul II. In his first encyclical, the Polish Pope announced that the aim of his ministry would be to direct the gaze of Church and world towards Christ the Lord, the Redeemer of Man. Wherever he travels, whatever dilemma he confronts, he bears the same Petrine message: *Christ is the key.* In this book I am inviting my readers to walk with John Paul the Key-Bearer through the doors that Christ alone unlocks. I want the Pope's message to be heard anew: 'The decisive answer to every one of man's questions, his religious and moral questions in particular, is given by Jesus Christ, or rather is Jesus Christ Himself'.[4] *Christ is the answer.*

Vicar of Christ, Witness to Christ

When he proclaims the Lord Jesus as the answer to all man's questions, Pope John Paul is doing what the New Testament calls 'bearing witness' to Christ. Just as Jesus bore witness to the truth (cf. John 18.37), the truth of the Father and of Himself as eternal Son,[5] so the Apostles bear witness by the power of the Holy Spirit (cf. John 15.26f.). From his Baptism, every Christian is called to be a witness of faith and the love of Christ – by word and by the good deeds of a holy life.[6] Confirmation gives him the special strength of the Holy Spirit to carry out that witness.[7] Ordination to the Apostolic Ministry equips the chosen Christian man to bear witness to Christ in an essentially different way – by being His consecrated icon and

[3] *Documentation Catholique* (1966), 2122.
[4] VS 2.
[5] St Augustine says of this text: 'When Christ bears witness, He really bears witness to Himself as He says, "I am the truth"' (*In Iohannis Evangelium Tractatus* 115, 2; CCSL 36. 644; cf. St Bede the Venerable, *In S. Joannis Evangelium Expositio*, cap. 18 (PL 92. 904D)).
[6] Cf. LG 10, 35; *Decreta*, pp. 110f., 158; CCC 905.
[7] Ibid., n. 11; p. 111; CCC 1303.

by acting in His person.[8] Teaching in communion with the Roman Pontiff, the bishops of the Church continue the witnessing work of the Apostles.[9] They are not *eye*-witnesses of the incarnate Word, but they are the successors of those who were (cf. 1 John 1.1ff.), and they sustain the apostolic testimony to Him through the ages. 'Every bishop', said Pope John Paul in 1985, 'is, in his Church, the teacher, the servant, and the witness of Christ the truth'.[10]

The head of the college of bishops, the Successor of St Peter, is the witness to Christ *par excellence*. What each bishop does for his particular Church, the Bishop of Rome is called to do for the Church universal, indeed for all mankind. In all his teaching, not only in those rare acts performed *ex cathedra*, the Pope has no other mission than this: to guard, proclaim, and unfold the Divine Revelation of which Christ is the fullness and mediator. 'The dispensation of truth abides', says St Leo the Great, 'and Blessed Peter, persevering in the strength he received, does not abandon the helm of the Church . . . Daily in the universal Church, Peter says, "You are the Christ, the Son of the living God"'.[11] Every Bishop of Rome has had the task of centring men on Christ, but some have been even more Christ-centred in their teaching than others in the sense that they have had to respond to specifically Christological errors.[12] This was true of many of the Roman Pontiffs of the first millennium, most notably St Leo I, and it is also true of the man who may be the last Pope of the second millennium, John Paul II.

In response to the needs of the time, Pope John Paul makes explicit what his predecessors were able to leave implicit. He has been called to show how everything in Christianity is from Christ and leads back to Christ and so to the Father in the Holy Spirit. It seems so obvious that without Christ there is no Christianity, and yet the obvious, for all its Himalayan prominence, has escaped the attention of many who claim the name 'Christian'. John Paul II has needed to be more expressly Christ-

[8] See chapter 13 below.
[9] Cf. LG 24, 25; *Decreta*, p. 137f.
[10] 14/5/85.
[11] *Tractatus* 3, 3; CCSL 138. 12f.
[12] For my definition of 'Christocentricity', see chapter 1.

centred than previous Popes because never before have sons of the Church rushed so furiously from the saving Centre. There are men and women marked by the Master (in Baptism or Ordination) who seem determined to disown Him (cf. 2 Peter 2.1), to preach other Christs, other Gospels (cf. 2 Cor. 11.4, Gal. 1.7), to search for new names by which they may be saved (cf. Acts 4.12). A 'Christianity without Christ' is under construction.

Pope John Paul has a Christological mission because, in this late twentieth century, Christological heresies long thought dead are being revived. Gnosticism and Pelagianism, in particular, are enjoying unprecedented success. The Gnostics of Christian antiquity denied the reality of the flesh which the Son of God took from Mary, and pretended that their own secret 'knowledge' was more salvific than the Blood of the Lamb. The Pelagians, though notionally orthodox in Christology,[13] also subverted man's need for the divine Redeemer: man is not wounded by an inherited Original Sin and does not need Christ's internal grace in order to be saved. For Gnostics and Pelagians alike, man can save himself by his own resources.

The Docetism of ancient Gnosticism – the belief that Christ only *seemed* to have a human body – is reproduced in the disdain of some contemporary theologians for the bodily aspects of Divine Revelation: the Virginity of the Lord's Mother, His Resurrection in the flesh, His Real Presence in the Eucharist.[14] The refusal of the feminists to ascribe any positive significance to the maleness of Jesus has led some of them to dust down the old Gnostic myth of an androgynous risen Christ.[15] Christological Docetism can also be detected in certain trends

[13] The Christology of the Pelagians is still largely unresearched. The support they received from Nestorius may signify a certain affinity between the two heresies. The Council of Ephesus (431) condemned both Nestorianism and Pelagianism.

[14] On modern Gnosticism, see Giandomenico Mucci SJ, 'Mito e periculo della Gnosi moderna', *La Civiltà Cattolica* (1992), 14–22.

[15] For example, Elizabeth A. Johnson has argued that Jesus' maleness is 'intrinsically important for his own historical identity and the historical challenge of his ministry, but not theologically determinative of his identity as the Christ' (*She Who is*. The Mystery of God in Feminist Theological Discourse (New York, 1992), p. 156). Johnson takes up the heresy of the Gnostic Cerinthus by claiming that 'Jesus' and 'the Christ' are not strictly the same person. The glorified Christ is 'a pneumatological reality, a creation [sic] of the Spirit who

in ecclesiology. At the end of the first century, St Ignatius of Antioch noticed that a Docetist view of Christ's individual body went hand in hand with an elitist and spiritualistic view of His Mystical Body. The Docetists believed that the 'true Church' was an invisible clique of superior 'knowing' people, and so they felt free to ignore the hierarchy, despise the poor, and shun what they saw as the coarse of materialism of the Mass. St Ignatius writes thus to the Church in Smyrna:

> They have no care for love, none for the widow, none for the orphan, none for the afflicted, none for the prisoner, none for the hungry or thirsty. They abstain from the Eucharist and from prayer, because they do not confess the Eucharist to be the flesh of our Saviour Jesus Christ, the flesh which suffered for our sins, and which the Father of His goodness raised up.[16]

Something similar is happening in our own time. Those who demand the right to dissent from the Magisterium appear embarrassed by the Catholic Church's claim that it is in her, this historically identifiable society, that the true Church of the God–Man is to be found. They seem shocked by the thought of creatures of flesh and blood teaching with the authority of Christ. They want an ethereal, a more academic Church, a club for discussing their own ideas rather than a Mother who teaches the truth of her Spouse. But the Word made flesh built His Church on a rock, not on the clouds, and He promised the guidance of the Holy Spirit not to professors but to fishermen and the bishops who succeed them. As Cardinal Ratzinger has said, 'the Church is not an idea but a Body, and the scandal of becoming flesh over which so many of Jesus' contemporaries

---

is not limited by whether one is Jew or Greek, slave or free, male or female' (p. 162). The conclusion is then drawn: 'Christ, in contrast to Jesus, is not male, or more exactly not exclusively male' (p. 162, quoting Sandra Schneiders with approval). The Resurrection, on Johnson's view, would appear to destroy Jesus in His bodily and male humanity and replace Him with the androgynous figure of 'the whole Christ'. For the obsession with androgyny in Gnosticism, see Werner Foerster, *Gnosis. A Selection of Gnostic Texts*, ET, vol. 1 (Oxford, 1972), p. 88 (the Ophites), p. 127 (Valentinus), and p. 263f. (the Naassenes). The fascination of contemporary feminism with Gnosticism is well illustrated in Karen L. King (ed.), *Images of the Feminine in Gnosticism* (Philadelphia, 1988).

[16] *Epistola ad Smyrnaeos* 6; J. B. Lightfoot (ed.), *The Apostolic Fathers*, vol. 2, section 1 (London, 1885), p. 306f.

stumbled continues in the scandalous character of the Church'.[17]
The Church, like her Head, is an incarnate reality.

A kind of Gnosticism is also evident in dissent from the
Church's moral teaching. The relativistic theologies eager to
defend contraception, abortion, and homosexual activity rest
on a Gnostic opposition between *bios* and *ethos*.[18] Once the
human body has been banished from its borders, the realm of
morality becomes a narrow angelistic republic of thoughts and
intentions.[19] Applying a perverse dualism, these moral
theologies make the human body extrinsic to the human person
and the human act.[20] They fail to perceive the body's nuptial
meaning, the language the divine Word first spoke in the
Virgin's womb when He wedded human flesh to Himself.[21]

Pelagianism, too, flourishes in the contemporary Church. Its
message is re-echoed in all the movements that preach the
possibility of fulfilment by one's own unaided efforts. For the
spiritualities touched by the 'New Age', fulfilment is an
individualistic 'wholeness' attained by psychic techniques of
enlightenment; for Liberation Theology, it is a collectivistic 'new
society' reached by political or social change. In both cases,
whether Nirvana or Utopia, it is the delusion of a deliverance
of man by man, not the God–Man.

[17] 'Die Ekklesiologie des Zweiten Vatikanischen Konzils', in *Kirche, Ökumene
und Politik*. Neue Versuche zur Ekklesiologie (Einsiedeln, 1987), p. 15.

[18] As Hans Urs von Balthasar has written: 'the Gnostic impulse secretly or
openly animates all those modern world-views which see "body" and "spirit",
bios and *ethos*, nature and God, in antagonism or opposition' (*The Scandal of the
Incarnation*. Irenaeus against the Heresies (San Francisco, 1990), p. 5).

[19] Cf. VS nn. 48ff.

[20] There is another chilling contemporary parallel with ancient Gnosticism.
St Epiphanius mentions a Gnostic sect which practised ritual abortion (*Adversus
Haereses* 1, 2 [26, 4]; PG 41. 340B).

[21] St John of the Cross follows the Fathers and St Thomas when he speaks of
the Hypostatic Union as a marriage of divinity and humanity in the Word. He
makes the eternal Son speak thus to the Father: 'I will go now and seek my
Bride,/And take upon my shoulders strong/The cares, the weariness, and
labours/Which she has suffered for so long./And that she may win new life/
I myself for her will die,/Rescue her from the burning lake,/And bear her
back to you on high' (*Romance* VII in St John of the Cross, *Poems*, ET by Roy
Campbell (Harmondsworth, 1960), p. 89). The 'Bride' here is humanity in both
the individual and universal sense: the human nature assumed by the Son,
and the human race which He embraces with a husbandly love.

The religion of the Word made flesh will always be folly to the world's wisdom.[22] The creature intent on glorifying itself resents the Creator who humbled Himself. That is why some theologians have suggested that Lucifer's sin was directed from the beginning against the Incarnation.[23] That, too, is why the Promethean philosophers of the last one hundred and fifty years have been not merely a-theistic, but anti-theistic, anti-Christian, anti-Christ.[24] In the late fourth century, St Augustine already understood this mentality. Before his conversion, he tells us, he was just too proud to accept the God who made Himself so small – the baby in the womb and arms of Mary, the dying man on the tree:

> I was not yet humble enough to hold the humble Jesus as my God, nor did I know what lesson His embracing of our weakness was to teach . . . [Your Word] built for Himself here below a humble house of clay. His intention was to bring down from themselves and bring up to Himself those to be made subject to Him. He wanted to heal the swollenness of their pride and nurture their love, so that they should no longer march forward in self-confidence, but might realize their weakness, when they saw the Deity at their feet, enfeebled by the taking of our coat of human nature. Then, weary at last, they would cast themselves down upon His humanity, and when it rose, so would they.[25]

[22] St Thomas Aquinas, who loved true wisdom, explains as follows why we must oppose evil wisdom, the wisdom of the world: 'There is an evil kind of wisdom . . . which is called "the wisdom of the world" (cf. 1 Cor. 2.6), because it takes some earthly good to be the highest cause and ultimate end' (2a2ae 46, 1, ad 2). The world's wisdom can even be called 'diabolical' because it imitates the pride of the devil (cf. 2a2ae 45, 1, ad 1).

[23] Suarez, for example, argued that Lucifer's pride is only comprehensible on the supposition that the future Incarnation of the Word was revealed to him when he was *in via*. He refused to obey a created will, even one existing in an uncreated Person. His pride is directed, therefore, from the beginning, against the humility of God in becoming man (*De Malis Angelis* in *Opera Omnia*, new ed., vol. 7 (Paris, 1857), p. 986). This is a problematic thesis, not least because of what it implies about the predestination of the Incarnation. However, the point Suarez is making about the specifically anti-Christian hatred of Satan remains valid.

[24] See Henri de Lubac, *The Drama of Atheistic Humanism*, ET (Cleveland & New York, 1963), p. vii.

[25] *Confessiones* 7, 18; CCSL 27. 108. The character Solly Lee in Caryll Householander's novel *The Dry Wood* (London, 1974) stands looking at a statue of the Madonna and Child, and suddenly he grasps what Christianity is about. 'He had never thought of Christianity in terms of a little Son, given to man. Now he saw it as just that' (p. 128).

Martyr for Christ

The Christian bears witness to Christ in a hostile environment. In St John's Gospel this order and atmosphere of opposition is called 'the world'; it is the unholy alliance of Satan ('the prince of this world') with sinful men who love self to the point of despising God.[26] On the eve of His Passion, our Lord foretold that the world in this negative sense would hate His disciples as it hated Him; indeed, it would persecute and kill them, as it persecuted and killed Him (cf. John 15.18–16.2). Thus the supreme witness, the testimony *par excellence*, is martyrdom. The very Greek word from which we get the English 'martyrdom' means 'witness', witness in blood. The martyr bears witness to Jesus, as Jesus bore witness to the Father, by laying down his life. He does not die for an abstract idea, but for a living person, the divine person of the Son of God, who loved him and gave Himself up for him (cf. Gal. 2.20). In Balthasar's words, the martyr dies in gratitude and praise, in 'a passion of responsive love'.[27] With St Ignatius of Antioch, the white-robed army all say: 'Leave me to imitate the Passion of my God'.[28] Martyrdom by blood is a gift given to the few. Nevertheless, for every Christian, it is a model of fidelity to Jesus.[29] As the Second Vatican Council teaches:

> Though the gift is given to few, all must nevertheless be ready to confess Christ before men and follow Him, on the way of the cross, through the persecutions which the Church never lacks.[30]

[26] It is important to distinguish the various meanings of 'world' (*kosmos*) in St John's Gospel. St Thomas lists them as follows: '"World" in Scripture can be taken in three ways. Sometimes it is taken from the point of view of its creation, as when the Evangelist says below, "The world was made through Him" (John 1.10). Sometimes it is taken from the point of view of its perfection, the perfection it attains through Christ, as in the text, "God was in Christ reconciling the world to Himself" (2 Cor. 5.19). And sometimes it is taken from the point of view of its perversity, as in the text, "The whole world lies under the power of the Evil One" (1 John 5.19)' (*Super Evangelium S. Ioannis Lectura* 5).

[27] Hans Urs von Balthasar, *New Elucidations*, ET (San Francisco, 1986), p. 288.

[28] *Epistola ad Romanos* 6; J. B. Lightfoot (ed.), *The Apostolic Fathers*, vol. 2, section 1 (London, 1885), p. 306f.

[29] This is argued by Balthasar in his little book, *Cordula oder der Ernstfall*, 4th ed. (Einsiedeln, 1987). See also p. 111 below.

[30] LG 42; *Decreta*, p. 172.

If the Pope enjoys a primacy of witness to Christ, he is also called to a primacy of martyrdom. His special Petrine powers – in teaching and jurisdiction – are not for his own glory; there is no 'primacy of honour' in Christianity. Everything that raises him above his brother bishops and fellow Christians is for the sake of service and at the cost of humiliation. He is lifted up in the way of the Son of Man was (cf. John 12.32): to be exposed to the scorn and hatred of an anti-Christian world.

Jesus gave Peter a share in His power. He strengthened him so that he could strengthen his brothers (cf. Luke 22.32). He established him as the rock on which He would build His Church, and handed him the Keys of the Kingdom (cf. Matt. 16.18f.). However, He also asked him to imitate His weakness, the victorious infirmity of the Cross:

> Truly, truly, I say to you, when you were young, you girded yourself and walked where you would; but when you are old, you will stretch out your hands, and another will gird you and carry you where you do not wish to go (John 21.18).

According to tradition, St Peter died a death of the utmost degradation, crucified head downwards because he deemed himself unworthy to die in the manner of the Lord.[31] The words of his colleague Paul describe Peter's own destiny: he who is first is made the last of all, a spectacle to the world, a fool for Christ's sake (cf. 1 Cor. 4.9). Peter is not strong despite his crucified weakness, but in it. It is when he is weak that he is strong (cf. 2 Cor. 12.10), because then the strength of Christ has the chance of working unimpeded by pride. 'My grace is sufficient for you, for my power is made perfect in weakness' (2 Cor. 12.9). In the office of Peter there is a permanent coincidence of authority and abasement. The faithful of Christ may cry *Viva il Papa*, but the man of the world shouts *Tolle, tolle, crucifige eum*. Balthasar sets forth the paradox as follows:

> When He conferred His office on Peter, Christ exhorted Peter to follow Him to the Cross, so that in the institutional Church the mission laid on the believer should be one with his surrender of his life; such identity would not have been Peter's ethical achievement, but rather an incomprehensible grace from the Lord

---

[31] Cf. Eusebius, *Historia Ecclesiastica* 3, 1; PG 20. 216A.

... Christ establishes the Petrine form upon this simultaneity, which is peculiar to institutional authority, of humiliation and elevation to office. This simultaneity is the mode in which the Lord's identity can (subsequently) still take hold of the guilty Peter. It is an imitation beyond and despite failure which is marvellously represented in Peter's crucifixion with feet uppermost: it is the Cross, but in mirror-image, which is the definitive symbol of the hierarchical situation.[32]

The first Pope died as a martyr, and so have many of his successors. The last Pope honoured as a martyr was St Martin I (649–653). Because of his fearless defence of the two natural wills of Christ against the Monothelite ('one will') heresy favoured by the Emperor Constans II, he was arrested and, though gravely ill, dispatched in chains to Constantinople. He endured solitary confinement, a show trial, public flogging, and then another grim sea-journey to the Crimea, where he died of hunger and the bitter cold. All this Martin suffered for the Catholic truth of Jesus, in the cause of Christological orthodoxy. Writing to John, Bishop of Philadelphia, whom he appointed as his vicar in the East, he gave beautiful expression to his Petrine vocation to witness:

I bear witness (diamartyromai) before God and Jesus Christ and the chosen angels, so that you may guard these things without prejudice ... With a pure conscience, hand on the Gospel of grace as you have received it from the holy Fathers and from Us, who have confirmed their teachings at a synod. Do not be ashamed of the witness (martyrion) of our Lord Jesus Christ, but be strengthened by His grace.[33]

Monothelitism, like Arianism earlier and Iconoclasm later, was the official policy of 'Caesaropapists', emperors who claimed supreme authority over the Church in both doctrine and discipline. It was not a tentative theory discussed by mild scholars, but a rigid ideology enforced by mailed soldiers. Though not all exhibited the courage of St Martin, many of the

[32] Hans Urs von Balthasar, *The Glory of the Lord: A Theological Aesthetics* I: Seeing the Form, ET (Edinburgh, 1982), p. 566f. St Peter is conformed to Christ, according to Balthasar, 'in inversion' (*Die antirömische Affekt. Wie lässt sich das Papstum in der Gesamtkirche integrieren* (Freiburg, 1974), p. 130).

[33] *Epistola* 5; PL 87. 162B.

Popes between the fourth and ninth centuries had to weather the fury of Caesaropapists. At the same time, the persecuted defenders of orthodoxy in the East, men like St Maximus the Confessor and St Theodore the Studite, looked to them not only for Petrine teaching and government, but also for a Petrine readiness to stand up against the princes of the world. The Papacy had primacy in martyrdom as well as Magisterium. When he was suffering at the hands of the Iconoclast emperors, St Theodore the Studite (759–826) appealed to Pope St Paschal I. He recognized that the Petrine Office gave Paschal a special share in Christ's power ('You have received from God the authority to be first of all'), but he also saw that it plunged him in a new way into the Lord's Passion: 'Good shepherd, we beseech you, lay down your life for your sheep'.[34]

In the sixteenth century a prince of England tried to lord it over a Pope of Rome, and once again, even in an age not famed for heroic virtue in the See of Peter, the Papacy was seen as a martyrological office. In 1534 Henry VIII was looking for approval from churchmen for his divorce and rebellion against Rome.[35] Bishop Sampson of Chichester dutifully preached in favour of the royal supremacy, but Reginald Pole, the king's kinsman, when his opinion was sought, wrote a treatise, specially for the king's eyes, on the Church's independence from the world. Pole argued that clerics such as Sampson were sad conformists, men of a worldly mentality who recognized no rule but the sword of a king; by the logic of their argument, Nero, not Peter, would have been visible head of the apostolic Church.[36] In contrast, the martyrs, such as 'those great men and dear to God', St John Fisher and St Thomas More, revealed the secret of the Church's world-resisting power: 'The power of all those to whom it is granted by Christ to suffer chains for Him is

[34] *Epistola* 2, 12; PG 99. 1152B–1153C.
[35] G. K. Chesterton said of Henry VIII: '[He] was a Catholic in everything except that he was not a Catholic . . . he accepted everything except Rome. And in that instant of refusal, his religion became a different religion, a different sort of thing' (*The Well and the Shallows*, in *Collected Works*, vol. 3 (San Francisco, 1990), p. 367). The 'anti-Roman complex' does not leave a man's faith intact.
[36] *Pro Ecclesiasticae Unitatis Defensione* (Rome, 1536), XA.

greater than royal power'.[37] According to Pole, the ministry of the Pope resembles the mission of the martyr. Cardinal Ratzinger has summarized the thinking as follows:

> The testimony that a person gives in the form of martyrdom verifies the witness he bears to Him who was both nailed to the Cross and victorious on the Cross. The primacy is primarily to be seen in this light – as a witness to Christ, a confession of Christ.[38]

Pole saw the Papacy as Balthasar does – as an office of humiliation, a particular kind of sharing in the self-emptying of Christ. He suggested that Isaiah's Christmas prophecy (chapter 9) could be applied to the Pope. The Son of God came into this world as a little child (cf. Isa. 9.6). The greatest became the least of all. That means that the Pope 'in the office of shepherd must regard himself and behave as the least and acknowledge that he knows nothing other than this alone, that he has been taught by God the Father through Christ (cf. 1 Cor. 2.2)'.[39] The titles of sovereignty listed by the prophet belong to Christ essentially as God, but the prophet ascribes them to Him as man, in the lowliness and littleness of His human childhood. Therefore, 'the only way a man can really share in Christ's majesty is to share in His abasement. In fact, abasement is the only way the majesty can be expressed and made present'.[40] The Chair on which Peter sits turns out to be the Cross.

On 13 May 1981, a gunman shot and wounded Pope John Paul in St Peter's Square. In the city where Peter was martyred, Peter's successor spilt his blood for Christ. He survived the attack, but he had made his testimony. Five months later, in a General Audience address, the Pope said that his suffering was a divine trial and his recovery a divine grace. Both trial and grace came to him not just as an individual man, but as the Bishop of Rome and Successor of St Peter. Through the sufferings of His Vicar, Jesus was teaching something, giving something, to His Church:

[37] Ibid., XVB.
[38] *Kirche, Ökumene und Politik*. Neue Versuche zur Ekklesiologie (Einsiedeln, 1987), p. 42f.
[39] Pole, cited by Ratzinger, op. cit., p. 45.
[40] Ratzinger, ibid., p. 45f.

Christ, who is the Light of the World, the Shepherd of His fold and, above all, the Prince of Pastors, has granted me the grace to be able, through suffering and at the risk of life and health, to bear witness to His Truth and to His Love ... How many successors of Peter in this Roman See have sealed this witness of pastoral and magisterial service with the sacrifice of their life? ... It is difficult to speak of these things without deep veneration, without interior anxiety ... I, too, feel my human weakness deeply – and therefore I repeat the Apostle's words confidently: *virtus in infirmitate perficitur*, 'My power is made perfect in weakness' (cf. 2 Cor. 12.9).[41]

The Pope was attacked on 13 May, the anniversary of Our Lady's first appearance to the children at Fatima. He is convinced that Our Lord saved his life through the intercession of the Blessed Mother. In his Act of Entrustment at Fatima on 13 May 1991, he addressed the Blessed Virgin as 'my Mother for ever and especially on 13 May 1981, when I felt your helpful presence at my side'.[42] Mary, too, is a mystery of divine power made perfect in weakness. The lowly Virgin from whom the Son of God took His frail flesh is Heaven's mighty Queen, the Mediatrix of Christ's risen power.

Conformity to Christ, Non-Conformity to the World
Pope John Paul has shown an unflagging readiness, whatever the dangers, to resist the world and its false wisdom.[43] The second chapter of his encyclical on Christian morality is prefaced with the words of St Paul: 'Do not be conformed to this world' (Rom. 12.2), a text he regularly quotes on his travels and applies to the Church's relationship to many different cultures. For example, in 1987, on one of his visits to the United

[41] 14/10/81. The figure of St Stanislaw (1036–1079), his predecessor in the see of Krakow, who fell beneath the sword of a king, has long been an inspiration to him. In 1979 he joined in the celebrations of the ninth centenary of the martyred bishop. He also wrote a beautiful poem on St Stanislaw (cf. *Collected Poems* (New York, 1982), pp. 169ff.). In *Crossing the Threshold of Hope*, the Holy Father says that the Pope will always be 'a sign that will be contradicted ... a challenge' ((New York, 1994), p. 11).

[42] See Timothy Tindal-Robertson, *Fatima, Russia, and Pope John Paul II* (Still River, 1992), *passim*. Cf. also *Crossing the Threshold of Hope*, p. 131f.

[43] See n. 22 above.

States, he spoke thus of the perils of uncritically endorsing one's culture:

> The culture of every age contains certain ambiguities, which reflect the inner tensions of the human heart, the struggle between good and evil. Hence the Gospel, in its continuing encounter with culture, must always challenge the accomplishments and assumptions of the age.[44]

On his various 'pilgrimages', he rises above the polite conventions of diplomacy to challenge social and political orthodoxies. In a still Communist Poland he declared: 'The exclusion of Christ from the history of man is an act against man'.[45] And in capitalist America, where 'the wisdom of the world' has made the killing of the unborn child a matter of 'free choice' and the suicide of the sick a 'valid option', the Pope has said bluntly: 'The ultimate test of your greatness is the way you treat every human being but especially the weakest and most defenceless ones'. America's great causes will succeed only 'if respect for life and its protection by the law is granted to every human being from conception until natural death'.[46]

The Pope's 'radical' critics describe him as 'conservative', and so he is, if by 'conservatism' one means Catholic orthodoxy, the determination to conserve the truth of Christ in all its splendour. This, after all, is his duty as Pope, as bishop, as Christian.[47] However, if 'conservative' implies a timid conformism or conventionality, then Pope John Paul is most certainly not a conservative, and his critics are not radical. The Pope's Christ-centred teaching is revolutionary, world-defying and world-transforming, while the theologies trumpeted as radical are

---

[44] New Orleans, 12/9/87. From this same period, we might also mention the Holy Father's message to Bishop Brown of Auckland: 'We must not fall into the temptation of identifying a Christian way of life with the customs generally accepted in modern society' (20/1/86). During the Marian Year, he warned religious not to be conformed to the world (cf. *Litterae Encyclicae*, n. 4). In an Angelus address on 15 February 1987 he spoke of 'sad concessions to the spirit of the age'.

[45] 2/6/79.

[46] Pope John Paul II, *The Pope Speaks to the American Church* (San Francisco, 1992), p. 360f.

[47] In praying for the Pope, the Roman Canon of the Mass prays also for 'all who hold and foster in orthodoxy the Catholic and Apostolic faith'.

without exception dull adaptations to the spirit of the age. There is no one less liberated than the theological liberal, tossed to and fro by the winds of ideology. As the Pope consistently teaches, it is not freedom that sets free, but truth (cf. John 7.32). Freedom itself needs liberating,[48] and that liberation is the work of the Spirit of Christ, the Spirit of Truth, in the Church. Left to themselves, our wayward minds and unruly hearts, wounded by Original Sin, are easily captured by worldly fads and fancies. That is why the Magisterium, authorized by Christ, 'is not a limitation for theologians, but a liberation, for it preserves them from subservience to changing fashions and binds them securely to the unchanging truth'.[49] As G. K. Chesterton said, 'the Catholic Church is the only thing which saves a man from the degrading slavery of being a child of his age'.[50]

Chesterton had sufficient girth of mind to realize that Christian orthodoxy is an invigorating open space, like the sea or the mountains, whereas heresy is always a prison, a suffocating cell. In 1908, one year after Pope St Pius X's encyclical *Pascendi*, he delivered his own broadside against Modernism. He knew that for the theological relativist there can only be one virtue: *fashion*. If there are no unchanging truths or moral absolutes, then all the poor Modernist can ever hope to be is 'up-to-date', 'progressive', 'innovative', and the only accusation he can fling against orthodoxy is that it is 'heavy, humdrum, and safe'. The truth, though, said Chesterton, is the exact opposite. Orthodoxy is the romance, the revolution, the principle of cultural renewal. Heresy always takes the line of appeasement; it wants the culture to stay just as it is:

There never was anything so perilous or so exciting as orthodoxy . . . The orthodox Church never took the tame course or accepted the conventions; the orthodox Church was never respectable. It would have been easier to have accepted the earthly power of the Arians. It would have been easy, in the Calvinistic seventeenth century, to fall into the bottomless pit of predestination . . . It is always easy to let the age have its head; the difficult thing is to

[48] Cf. VS 86.
[49] Maynooth, 1/10/79.
[50] *The Catholic Church and Conversion* in G. K. Chesterton, *Collected Works*, vol. 3 (San Francisco, 1990), p. 110.

keep one's own. It is always easy to be a Modernist; as it is easy to be a snob. To have fallen into any of those open traps of error and exaggeration which fashion after fashion and sect after sect set along the historic path of Christendom – that would indeed have been simple. It is always simple to fall; there are an infinity of angles at which one falls, only one at which one stands. To have fallen into any one of the fads from Gnosticism to Christian Science would indeed have been obvious and tame. But to have avoided them all has been one whirling adventure; and in my vision the heavenly chariot flies thundering through the ages, the dull heresies sprawling and prostrate, the wild truth reeling but erect.[51]

The Christ-centred orthodoxy of Pope John Paul, like Catholic orthodoxy in every age, is 'wild truth', a revolutionary truth that will turn the Satan-ruled world upside down. Christ our centre is the conqueror of sin and death, the Harrower of Hell. That is why even in this life, in his non-conformity to the world, the orthodox believer can know joy, 'the gigantic secret of the Christian'.[52] 'Be of good cheer', says the Lord, 'I have overcome the world' (John 16.33). The world may do its worst, and yet whatever pain it inflicts has already been borne, ahead of us, by the Head of us – the incarnate Son of God. When we enter the world of suffering, we find that it is already in the Heart of Jesus, offered to His Father and transfigured in His risen body. As the Swiss mystic Adrienne von Speyr, for whom the Pope has a great admiration, says in her commentary on St John's Gospel:

> They should be of good cheer, because all the suffering that will overtake them will bear the mark of authenticity: it has been known, determined, and suffered in advance by the Lord. And in so far as all possible suffering is included within His own suffering, He has overcome the world. He overcame it on the Cross, where He died in total loneliness as the conquered one, forsaken by all. And yet He accomplished His task, and when He dies, He can take the mission He has accomplished back to the Father. He does not say 'I will overcome the world', for He has already overcome it . . .[53]

[51] G. K. Chesterton, Collected Works, vol. 1 (San Francisco, 1986), p. 305f.
[52] Cf. Chesterton, Orthodoxy, p. 365.
[53] Adrienne von Speyr, Die Abschiedsreden. Betrachtungen über Johannes 13–17 (Einsiedeln, 1948), p. 395f.

Christ is the Head of all men. His victory over the hostile world is our victory. In our flesh He suffered and died, and in that same flesh He rose again, ascended into Heaven, and sits at the Father's right hand. Even now His glorious body bears the scars of His Passion, and from His body, through the scars, power goes forth into the Sacraments, to renew and transform us in His likeness.[54] Thus we have hope. The Son has made a place for us in His Father's house. Where the Head has gone, the members by His grace may also go. The Word made flesh is the centre of history, but He is also its goal, man's final happiness, our undying joy, our Heaven.[55]

This book is an introduction to Christ and Christianity based on the teaching of the man Roman Catholics believe to be the Vicar of Christ and the Teacher of All Christians. For Roman Catholics, I hope it will strengthen their faith in the incarnate Word and confirm their belief that the Papacy is His gift. For Protestants, especially those anxious about the trend to secularism in their denominations, it is intended to show that the elements in Catholicism that they usually see as a distraction from Christ (Marian devotion, the Papacy) actually come from Him and lead to Him. I hope that it will inspire all its Christian readers to a more ardent conformity to Christ in faith and charity and a bolder non-conformity to the world. I pray that it will fill the hearts of all who read it with the joy of the risen and conquering Son and deepen their longing to see Him in His glory. 'In the world', says the Lord, 'you have tribulation; but be of good cheer, I have overcome the world' (John 16.33).

---

[54] *The Catechism of the Catholic Church* includes as an illustration a fresco from the catacombs showing Jesus with the woman with the flow of blood (cf. Luke 8.43ff.). It comments: 'The Sacraments of the Church now continue the works that Christ carried out during His life on earth. The Sacraments are like "powers coming forth" from the Body of Christ to heal us of the wounds of sin and to give us the new life of Christ' (French edition (Paris, 1992), p. 230).

[55] 'Heaven ... must first and foremost be determined Christologically' (Joseph Ratzinger, *Eschatology. Death and Eternal Life*, ET (Washington, 1988), p. 234). As St Ambrose says of the Penitent Thief, 'life is being with Christ. Where Christ is, there is the Kingdom' (*Expositio Evangelii secundum Lucam* 10, 121; CCSL 14. 379).

The world. This world, in which man lives,
in which man rules,
this world which in the final analysis seems to conquer man.
It conquers him through death.
But Christ, who has conquered death, has conquered the
world . . .
'The world', through the whisper of the original Lie,
became in man's heart the adversary of God,
began to banish God from the human heart . . .
Where He conquers death,
Christ reveals the world anew to man;
this world, which banished God from man's heart,
is given back by Christ to God and to man
as the place of the original Covenant,
which must also be the definitive covenant
when God will be all in all . . .
Man of our day!
You, man, who live immersed in the world and think you are its
master
while perhaps you are its prey,
Christ frees you from every form of slavery
in order to propel you towards self-conquest,
            towards love . . .
Christ sets you free because He loves you,
because He has given Himself up for you,
because He has conquered for you and for all.
Christ has restored the world and you to God.
He has restored God to you and to the world.
Forever!
'Be of good cheer, I have overcome the world!'[56]

---

[56] Pope John Paul's Message *Urbi et Orbi*, Easter Sunday, 15/4/90.

PART I

Christ the Centre

1

The Meaning of 'Christocentricity'

The Definition of Christocentricity

'Christocentricity' is defined by the *Oxford English Dictionary* as 'the state of having Christ as the Centre'. In its first and broadest meaning, it is a geometrical metaphor for that most fundamental attribute of Christian faith: belief in the uniqueness of Jesus Christ. As a circle has but one centre, so Jesus Christ, the incarnate Word, true God and true man, is absolutely singular, the only way to the Father, the human race's only Saviour.[1] The Pope's teaching is Christocentric in this sense, but then so is any theology deserving of the name 'Christian'.[2]

We need a narrower definition. Within the category of authentically Christian theologies, we must be able to determine degrees of centredness on Christ. In what follows, Christocentricity will be interpreted more strictly as a particular application of the analogy of faith. It is the emphasizing or making explicit of the *nexus mysteriorum*, the connection of each revealed truth with the person, life, teaching, and redemptive work of Jesus Christ. It is a habit of theological perception, seeing and then tracing the lines which run from the circumference of the Church's faith to Christological centre. The teaching of the Second Vatican Council is Christocentric in this strict sense. As Cardinal Razinger has said, summarizing its

[1] In *La Vita Nuova*, Dante makes Love say: 'I am like the centre of a circle, to which the parts of the circumference relate in similar fashion. You are not so' (n. 12).

[2] On the uniqueness of Christ, see pp. 103ff. below.

1

ecclesiology, 'Lumen gentium sit Christus. Because Christ is the light of the nations, there exists a mirror of His glory, the Church, that reflects His radiance'.[3] The Church is Christ's Church. Holy Church is His creation, and her teachings are His own. The Council's theology of revelation is also Christocentric; it is an example of 'Christological concentration'.[4] The first chapter of Dei Verbum sees the Word incarnate Himself as 'both the mediator and plenitude of all revelation'.[5] As Archbishop (now Cardinal) Zoungrana said, speaking in the name of sixty-nine African bishops, 'Tell the world that divine revelation is Christ. The beautiful face of Christ must shine more clearly in the Church'.[6]

My definition of Christocentricity is deliberately Catholic, by which I mean that it presupposes that the circle of revelation is a whole; the centre is indissolubly joined to all other points within its radius.[7] By contrast, the Protestant attempt at Christocentricity breaks the circle. Christ is separated from His Church, His Mother and His saints. Faith is cut off from charity. There is grace, but no co-operation; divine initiative, but no handmaidenly Yes.[8] Pope John Paul's Christocentricity is, by contrast, fully Catholic. As I hope to show, it is at once Marian, ecclesial, Eucharistic. Christ's singularity is not solitude. No creature can rival the glory of the risen Morning Star, but He does not shine alone; a whole constellation reflects His brightness. As Balthasar has said so beautifully, 'Christ does not live alone in His Church; He is accompanied by all the saints who fill heaven, and will never more be separated from

---

[3] J. Ratzinger, Kirche, Ökumene und Politik. Neue Versuche zur Ekklesiologie (Einsiedeln, 1987), p. 14.

[4] The phrase is Karl Barth's and is cited by Henri de Lubac in his commentary on Dei Verbum (La Révélation divine (Paris, 1983), p. 46).

[5] DVb 2; Decreta, p. 424.

[6] Cited in H. de Lubac, Entretien autour de Vatican II. Souvenirs et réflexions (Paris, 1985), p. 51.

[7] On the wholeness and completeness that is Catholicity, see Hans Urs von Balthasar, In the Fullness of Faith. On the Centrality of the Distinctively Catholic, ET (San Francisco, 1988), p. 13 and passim.

[8] On the difference between 'the Catholic And' and Protestantism's exclusions and oppositions, see Balthasar, Der antirömische Affekt. Wie lässt sich das Papsttum in der Gesamtkirche integrieren (Freiburg, 1974), pp. 248ff., and Karl Barth, Darstellung und Deutung seiner Theologie (Einsiedeln, 1976), pp. 335ff.

All of us shine the face of Christ. All Angels in Heaven, all saints in Heaven. Christ does not shine alone.

them'.[9] Christocentrism is not Christomonism. The central Christ is not a solitary.

Some Classics of Christocentricity

The Pope's teaching is truly his own. He writes a large part of his own encyclicals and arranges them in a coherent pattern. For his official work as teacher of all Christians, he draws on his personal gifts as poet, dramatist, philosopher and spiritual theologian. Of course, in the providence of God, as Balthasar has reminded us, things might have been different:

> After all, we could have an entirely different Pope, who might not be a philosopher, and yet could state the tenets of our faith in quite a simple manner. To what degree is the personal philosophy and theology of the Holy Father authoritative for the universal Church? I think his teachings expressly contain theses which are central to the understanding of our faith: the body, for instance, the human person, the community, and the wonderful things he has to say on human labour and divine mercy. What is developed here is rooted directly in revelation, and should be pondered by every Christian, not in order to construct a closed system with his encyclicals, but to obtain from his great intuitions a point of departure from which new reflections on divine revelation may emerge.[10]

Since Pope John Paul II's teaching has such a strongly personal stamp, it is important to show its continuity with the great Tradition of the Church. Before discussing his own version, we shall consider some earlier 'classics of Christocentricity': two medieval, one from the age of Baroque, a fourth from our own times.

St Bonaventure: Christ the Centre

Josef Seifert and Kenneth Schmitz have detected the influence of St Bonaventure on Karol Wojtyla.[11] No theologian has more

---

[9] Balthasar, *In the Fullness of Faith*, p. 116.

[10] *Test Everything: Hold Fast to What is Good*. An interview with Hans Urs von Balthasar by Angelo Scola, ET (San Francisco, 1989), p. 65.

[11] On St Bonaventure's influence on Wojtyla, see Josef Seifert, 'Karol Cardinal Wojtyla (Pope John Paul II) as Philosopher and the Cracow/Lublin School of Philosophy', *Aletheia* 2 (1981), 130–199, cited in Kenneth Schmitz, 'Karol Wojtyla's Anthropology: From the Lublin Lectures to *The Acting Person*' (unpublished), p. 6 n. 11. On Christ the Middle, see *In Hexaëmeron* 1, 10; *Opera*

systematically applied the imagery of centrality to Christ than the Sepharic Doctor. Our Lord Jesus Christ, he says, 'in all things holds the central position'. First, He is the 'Middle Person' (*media persona*) of the Trinity.[12] As the Second Person (the produced-producing Son), He is between the First (the unproduced-producing Father) and the Third (the produced-unproducing Spirit).[13] Even in His divinity, the uncreated Word is 'central' to creation, because He is the Art of the Father, expressing the Father and all He can do, all He wills to do.[14] By becoming man without ceasing to be God, He has become the 'middle' in another sense; He is the one Mediator between God and man, the centre of human history and the whole cosmos.[15] At every stage of His human life on earth, He is *in medio*: lying in the manger in the midst of the animals, sitting in the Temple in the midst of the doctors, serving in the midst of the disciples, hanging on the gibbet in the midst of thieves, standing resurrected in the midst of the Apostles.[16] Just as physical life is poured out from the heart, in the middle of the body, to the other limbs and organs, 'so Christ, crucified in the midst of thieves, the Tree of Life planted by God in the middle of Paradise (that is, the Church Militant), in the Sacraments pours the life of grace into the members of the Mystical Body'.[17]

Omnia t. V (Quaracchi, 1891), 330B. He is particularly attached to Bonaventure's way of asserting the inseparability of theology and holiness: 'Let no one think that it is enough for him to read if he lacks devotion' (*Itinerarium Mentis in Deum*, Prol.4; Quaracchi V, 296). This has been quoted many times (e.g. 25/4/79, 4/5/87, and in PDV 53). In his letter to the Minister General of the Franciscan families on the fourth centenary of the proclamation of St Bonaventure as a Doctor of the Church (8/9/88), he quoted the Christocentric maxim in the prologue to the *Itinerarium*: 'From Christ we come, by Him we live, and to Him we are directed' (n. 2). Moreover, St Bonaventure provides the Holy Father with one of his definitions of conscience in *Veritatis Splendor* (n. 58).

[12] *Commentarium super librum III Sententiarum* dist. 1, art. 2, quaest. 3, f. 1; Quaracchi III, 29A.

[13] *In Hexaëmeron* 1, 14; V, 331B.

[14] Ibid., 1, 13; V, 331B.

[15] Ibid., 1, 10 & 20; V, 330B & 332B.

[16] *Dominica infra octavam Epiphaniae, sermo* 7; IX, 177Af.

[17] *Dominica III Adventus, sermo* 1; IX, 57Bf.

St Thomas Aquinas: Christ the Only Way

Pope John Paul II has often repeated the teaching of his predecessors about the privileged place of St Thomas Aquinas in the study of philosophy and theology. For example, the encyclical *Veritatis Splendor* reaffirms St Thomas's general doctrine of natural law[18] as well as his view that 'the morality of the human act depends on the "object" rationally chosen by the rational will'.[19]

The Pope is without doubt a Thomist, but not an archaeological one. He is not content merely to expound St Thomas's thought; he wants also to prove its vitality and resourcefulness, its capacity to accommodate new insights into reality. The supervisor of his doctoral studies in Rome, Father Reginald Garrigou-Lagrange OP, though regarded as a conservative Thomist, showed the future Pope the possibility of integrating the philosophy and theology of St Thomas with the mystical doctrine of St John of the Cross. On his return to Poland, during the early 1950s, the then Father Wojtyla joined several other young philosophers at the Catholic University of Lublin in trying to develop a new kind of Thomism.[20] Having recently witnessed the Nazi attempt to overthrow the objective moral order, they were determined not to fall into subjectivism or idealism; on the other hand, they wanted at all costs to avoid the Marxist materialism which was now oppressing the Polish spirit. Man was their proper subject, but not man on his own; they realized that a man-centred doctrine of man could only be destructive of man. As the Polish poet Cyprian Norwid said, 'humanity without the divine betrays herself'.[21] The Lublin Thomists wanted a Christian, truly God-centred humanism.

---

[18] VS n. 44.

[19] Ibid., n. 78. Cf. n. 24.

[20] Cf. Andrew N. Woznicki, 'Lublinism – A New Version of Thomism', *Proceedings of the American Catholic Philosophical Association* (1986), 23–37. The man often regarded as the head of the Lublin school is Mieczyslaw Albert Krapiec OP. See his *I-Man. An Outline of Philosophical Anthropology* (New Britain, 1983), p. xvii. See also Edward Nieznanski's description of the different species of Polish Thomism in Emerich Coreth SJ *et al.* (edd.), *Christliche Philosophie im katholischen Denken des 19. und 20. Jahrhunderts*, vol. 2 (Graz, Vienna & Cologne, 1988), pp. 804ff.

[21] Cited by Woznicki (citing Stefan Swiezawski), p. 24.

The 'Existential Thomism' of Jacques Maritain and Etienne Gilson provided them with the first signposts, but they were soon marching off in new directions. In the case of Karol Wojtyla, the journey led him to the work of Max Scheler and to what he has called the 'modest' task of combining a Thomist philosophy of being with a phenomenological philosophy of consciousness.

Lublin Thomism has given the Pope some refreshingly original insights into the theology of St Thomas. In an address in 1979, at a celebration of the centenary of *Aeterni Patris*, he linked the Angelic Doctor with his own Christocentric vision in *Redemptor Hominis*. Some will find this association problematic, since the theology of St Thomas may appear to be insufficiently Christocentric in the strict sense defined above. However, closer consideration confirms the Holy Father's judgement. St Thomas has every right to take his place alongside his Franciscan colleague as a Christocentric theologian.

St Thomas's theology is both Christocentric and theocentric, indeed Trinitarian. Theology of its nature is centred on God, but Christ as man is the way to God,[22] and, of course, He is Himself God, God the Son made man, the only way to the Father:

> Faith is a foretaste of the knowledge that makes us happy in the future . . . Now the Lord taught that this beatifying knowledge consists in knowing two things – the Godhead of the Trinity and the manhood of Christ. As Christ said, addressing the Father, 'This is eternal life that they know thee the only true God, and Jesus Christ, whom thou has sent' (John 17.3). The whole knowledge of the faith, therefore, revolves round these two things – the Godhead of the Trinity and the manhood of Christ. This is not surprising, because the manhood of Christ is the way by which one goes to the Godhead.[23]

The *Summa* is devoted to God (questions 2–43 of the First Part), Man (questions 72–102 of the First Part and the whole of

[22] My reflections on the Christocentricity of St Thomas are indebted to Fr-M. Léthel, *Connaitre l'amour du Christ qui surpasse toute connaissance: La théologie des saints* (Venasque, 1989), pp. 221–298. On Christ as the way to God, see ST 1a 1, 2, prol.

[23] *Compendium Theologiae* 2.

the Second Part), and Christ (the Third Part). The Third Part is last but by no means least. It is the true climax of the whole work. Its point and purpose is to show that it is in and by the Word Incarnate, through the Sacraments of His Church, that man is brought into union with the Trinity in grace and glory. Moreover, since it is the questions on the Blessed Sacrament which form the last complete treatise of the *Summa*, it can be seriously argued that its pinnacle is not simply Christ but the Eucharistic Christ. As Father Léthel has written:

One might say that the saint's last act was to place the Blessed Sacrament in his unfinished cathedral; it was necessary for this architecture of light to be illumined from within by the Eucharistic Sun.[24]

Finally, a good case can be made for the view that St Thomas's anthropology in the *Summa* is presented in a Christological frame. Man (at the end of the First Part and in the Second Part) is enveloped by the one Lord Jesus Christ: in the mysteries of His divinity (in the First Part), and in the mysteries of His humanity (in the Third Part).[25]

Bérulle: Christ the Central Sun
It has been argued that the Christocentricity of medieval theology had a decisive influence on the development of modern science. Although they accepted the ancient cosmology, in which the earth is the centre of the material universe, the Church Fathers, followed by St Bonaventure and the other great theologians of the Middle Ages, saw Jesus Christ as both sun, the Sun of Justice, and centre, a dual function which was an astronomical solecism but a theological necessity. This is reflected in Dante's *Divine Comedy*, where, in the poet's three visions in Paradise, Christ is the central light, 'thousands of lamps surmounting, one sun which all and each enkindled'.[26]

Cardinal Pierre de Bérulle, whom Pope Urban VIII called 'the Apostle of the Word Incarnate', takes up the cosmological

---

[24] Léthel, p. 223.
[25] Ibid., p. 234.
[26] On medieval Christocentricity and the development of astronomy, see William Anderson, *Dante the Maker* (New York, 1982), p. 403; and James J. Collins, *Dante: Layman, Prophet, Mystic* (New York, 1989), p. 264.

image inherited from the Middle Ages. By placing the incarnate Son of God at the centre of his spiritual theology, Bérulle saw himself as effecting a kind of 'Copernican revolution'. In contrast to the more abstract tendency of some of the Christocentrisms of more recent times (for example, that of Teilhard de Chardin), Bérulle is emphatic that the fiery star at the core of the cosmos is none other than Jesus, the Word incarnate, in His real historical humanity, the Jesus of Bethlehem and Calvary and the altar:

> One of the outstanding minds of our times [Copernicus] maintains that the sun, and not the earth, is at the centre of the world . . . this novel opinion, little followed in the science of the stars, is useful and must be followed in the science of salvation. For Jesus is the sun, immobile in His grandeur and moving all things . . . Jesus is the true centre of the world, and the world must be in a continual movement towards Him. Jesus is the sun of our souls, from whom they receive all graces, lights and influences.[27]

Father Bourgoing, third General of the Oratory, in his preface to the works of Bérulle, compares the latter's Christocentric mission to that of John the Baptist. His whole apostolate was 'to point out Jesus Christ, to make Him known in the world, and not only His mysteries, His actions, His words, His miracles and sufferings, but also His person, His adorable states and grandeurs, to make Him revered, served, worshipped, and loved, and to form in us the living image of His life'.[28]

Like Bonaventure and Thomas, Bérulle is never exaggeratedly Christocentric, never Christomonistic. He sees Jesus always in His diverse states and thus in His several relations, divine and human: in the bosom of the heavenly Father, in the womb of the Holy Virgin, in the Blessed Sacrament of the altar. Anticipating the later 'mystery theology' of Odo Casel, he argues that, through the permanence of the wounds in the risen body of Jesus, all His earthly human actions and experiences, though concluded as events, remain as models and specific sources of grace for His members.[29]

[27] Bérulle, *Oeuvres complètes*, ed. J. P. Migne (Paris, 1856), p. 161.
[28] Ibid., p. 97.
[29] They are 'past with regard to performance, but they are present with regard to power' (ibid., 1052).

Hans Urs von Balthasar: the Splendour of Christ the Truth

Pope John Paul II has on several occasions expressed his admiration for the late Hans Urs von Balthasar, the twentieth-century Catholic theologian who more than any other deserves the epithet 'Christocentric'.[30] In 1984, in presenting Balthasar with the Paul VI International Prize, he praised him for 'placing his vast knowledge at the service of an *intellectus fidei* which would be able to show man the splendour of the truth which flows from Jesus Christ'.[31] A year later he addressed the symposium on the ecclesial mission of Adrienne von Speyr. He said that he was 'very pleased' with its work and linked Adrienne with the Rhineland mystics of the Middle Ages. He concluded by congratulating Balthasar on his eightieth birthday: 'I thank him once again for his immense theological work'.[32] Finally, in 1988 the Holy Father nominated Balthasar as a Cardinal. 'We would very gladly have seen him numbered among the Cardinals and lavished with our congratulations and marks of esteem.' It was not to be. Balthasar died suddenly two days before the consistory.[33]

There is no doubt that Balthasar was admired by John Paul II. But has his theology influenced papal teaching in any way? In particular, does the Pope's Christocentricity owe anything to this modern Father of the Church? The first, more general question can be answered directly and simply. In the major documents of his pontificate, the Holy Father, like his predecessors, is discreet in his citation of contemporary authors. Most references are to Scripture, to the Fathers, and to the Magisterium. However, in his Apostolic Letter on the dignity and vocation of women, *Mulieris Dignitatem*, the Pope quotes Balthasar to support the idea that the Church is 'both Marian and Apostolic-Petrine'.[34] Moreover, the phrase used by the

[30] See G. Marchesi SJ, *La Christologia di Hans Urs von Balthasar. La figura di Gesù Cristo espressione visibile di Dio* (Rome, 1977), pp. 48ff.
[31] 23/6/84.
[32] 28/9/85.
[33] 28/6/88.
[34] MD 27; AAS 80 (1988), 1718n. In his book *Crossing the Threshold of Hope*, the Holy Father mentions Balthasar as one of those 'great thinkers in the Church' who have been 'disturbed' by 'the problem of hell' ((New York, 1994), p. 185).

Pope above in applauding Balthasar's work – 'the splendour of truth', a phrase which recalls Balthasar's *Herrlichkeit* – is the title of the great encyclical on morality, *Veritatis Splendor*. John Paul II has the poet's sense of beauty, the dramatist's absorption in the struggle of goodness with evil, and the philosopher's devotion to truth. It is not surprising, therefore, that he should have felt drawn towards Balthasar, the architect of the 'Theological Aesthetic', 'Theodrama', and 'Theologic'. As for the question of Balthasar's influence on John Paul's Christocentricity, that will be answered *passim* throughout this book as I invoke Balthasar to illustrate the various aspects of the Pope's thinking.

2

Pope John Paul's Christocentricity

The fact of Pope John Paul's Christocentricity is easily proved. The opening words of his first encyclical state the truth upon which all his teaching is built: 'The Redeemer of man, Jesus Christ, is the centre of the universe and of history'.[1] Later in the same document the language of vision is used, suggesting that Christocentricity is a form of contemplation, a directing of the soul's eyes towards the incarnate Word:

> Our spirit is set in one direction; the only direction for our intellect, will and heart is towards Christ our Redeemer, towards Christ, the Redeemer of man. We wish to look towards Him – because there is salvation in no one else but Him, the Son of God – repeating what Peter said: 'Lord, to whom shall we go? You have the words of eternal life'.[2]

The gazing at Christ to which the Pope calls us is not cold outward observation. We are invited to look and let ourselves be transported. In words reminiscent of Balthasar's 'theological aesthetic', the act of faith is defined as 'letting oneself be enchanted by the luminous figure (*doxa*) of Jesus the revealer and by the love (*agape*) of Him who sent Him'.[3] The Pope is here speaking of what Balthasar calls the 'objective rapture' of faith-perception. In *The Glory of the Lord* Balthasar writes as follows:

[1] RH 1; AAS 71 (1979), 257. See also the Pope's book, *Crossing the Threshold of Hope* (New York, 1994), p. 44f.
[2] RH 7, 268.
[3] 15/10/98.

11

Even in the realm of worldly beauty, form cannot really be perceived without the beholder being taken up into it. The beautiful is never a mere flat surface; it always has heights and depths [4]

In the case of the 'Christ-form', mediated in Scripture and the Sacraments of the Church, the glorious 'heights and depths' to which the Holy Spirit transports us are Trinitarian, 'the love of Him who sent Him'.

All John Paul's first words and actions as Pope were centred on Christ: the first utterance at the end of the conclave, the first homily, the message of his first pilgrimage overseas. In *Redemptor Hominis*, the Holy Father disclosed that, in the act of accepting his canonical election, he entrusted himself anew to Christ. 'With obedience in faith to Christ, my Lord, and with trust in the Mother of Christ and of the Church, in spite of great difficulties, I accept.'[5] He wanted these words to be published to emphasize the 'link between the first fundamental truth of the Incarnation . . . and the ministry that, with my acceptance of my election as Bishop of Rome and Successor of the Apostle Peter, has become my specific duty in his See'.[6] The Petrine Office is of its very nature objectively Christocentric. From the first moments of his ministry, John Paul II has tried to make that Christocentricity more radiantly clear.

The homily at his inaugural Mass on 22 October 1978, began with a renewal of Peter's confession – 'You are the Christ, the Son of the Living God' (Matt. 16.16) – and included this prayer:

> Christ, make me become and remain the servant of your power that knows no eventide. Make me a servant, indeed, the servant of your servants.[7]

Having centred himself on Christ in prayer, he appealed to the men and women of the world to 'open wide the doors for Christ'.[8] These words have been the refrain of the pontificate,

[4] Balthasar, *The Glory of the Lord. A Theological Aesthetics*, vol. 1: Seeing the Form, ET (Edinburgh, 1982), p. 604.
[5] RH 2, 259.
[6] 22/10/78.
[7] Ibid.
[8] Ibid.

taken up in the great encyclicals and made the leitmotif of the Jubilee of Redemption in 1983.[9] The image in the Pope's mind seems to be the night visitor of the Apocalypse, represented unforgettably by Holman Hunt in 'The Light of the World': 'Behold, I stand at the door and knock; if any one hears my voice and opens the door, I will come in to him and eat with him, and he with me' (Apoc. 3.20). The refulgent Son of the Father comes to scatter the darkness of our hearts. So 'do not be afraid to welcome Christ and accept His power . . . Do not be afraid. Open wide the doors for Christ!'[10]

Pope John Paul's first pilgrimage overseas was in January 1979 to Latin America, to the Dominican Republic and thence to Puebla, Mexico, for the General Assembly of Latin American Bishops. His Puebla message, delivered with dramatic passion, was Christ-centred. He appealed to the bishops to guard bravely and to expound faithfully the full Christology of the Church. Without it, there could be no evangelization, for Jesus is Himself the Good News we preach:

> From you, pastors [= bishops of Latin America], the faithful of your countries expect and demand above all a careful and zealous transmission of the truth concerning Jesus Christ. This truth is at the centre of evangelization and constitutes its essential content.[11]

He repeated Peter's confession and then added: 'This in a certain sense is the only Good News: the Church lives by it and for it'.[12] He had come to Latin America to call for 'a solid Christology', to warn against 'the passing over in silence of Christ's divinity', interpretations that are 'at variance with the Church's faith', re-readings that are 'brilliant' but no more than 'fragile and inconsistent hypotheses'.[13] Against these he re-affirmed the Church's faith: 'Jesus Christ, the Word and the Son of God, becomes man in order to come close to man and to offer him, through the power of His mystery, salvation, the great gift of God'.[14]

[9] See the Bull *Aperite Portas Redemptori*: AAS 75 (1983), 89ff.
[10] 22/10/78.
[11] 28/1/79.
[12] Ibid.
[13] Ibid.
[14] Ibid.

The Year 2000

Pope John Paul has an extraordinary sense of occasion. No pontificate has seen so many official commemorations – of councils and encyclicals, of the birthdays and deaths of saints, of the conversion of nations. One date, though, from the beginning of his ministry, has been its special focus – the year 2000. Its significance is not mathematical but Christological. The date 'will recall and re-awaken in us in a special way our awareness of the key truth of faith which St John expressed at the beginning of his Gospel: "The Word became flesh and dwelt among us" (John 1.14)'.[15] The Marian Year took the form of an Advent of preparation for this bi-millennial jubilee of the Incarnation.[16]

The Holy Father's calendrical sensitivity derives from a Christocentric philosophy of time. For him, as for Balthasar, God-made-man is 'the norm of history'.[17] When the eternal Word enters into time, history's true meaning is revealed. Light falls from the centre on beginning and end. To set one's sights on the dawning third millennium is therefore an act of faith and hope in the Word made flesh, 'a renewed orientation of our history' towards Him who is Alpha and Omega.[18]

---

[15] RH 1, 258.
[16] RM 3; AAS 79 (1987), 363f.
[17] *A Theology of History*, ET (London & Sydney, 1964), *passim*.
[18] 22/10/78.

PART II

The Whole Christ

3

'You are Christ':
The Confession of Peter

The Papacy is of its nature objectively Christocentric. It is the gift of Jesus Christ: by Him it was instituted; by His Spirit it is assisted. Its teaching is unfailingly Christocentric. In every age Peter through his successors says, 'You are the Christ, the Son of the living God'. *The Pope is the first teacher of Christology in the Church.* At certain times this has been dramatically evident. One thinks, for example, of St Leo the Great acclaimed by the Fathers of Chalcedon ('Peter has spoken through Leo'), and of St Martin I, the last martyr Pope, who died for the truth of Christ's two natural wills and operations.

Not since the Patristic age has a Pope devoted himself so single-mindedly to the exposition of the church's Christology. As we have already seen, in *Redemptor Hominis* he links the institution of the Papacy with the Incarnation. His thinking may have been influenced by Vladimir Soloviev, the 'Russian Newman', who saw the visibility of the Petrine Office as an application of the sacramental principle established by the Incarnation.[1] The invisible Word was made visible flesh, and He built His Church on a readily recognizable office – the ministry of Peter and his successors.

[1] 'The Resurrection of Jesus Christ in the flesh has proved that bodily existence is not excluded from the union of the human and the divine, and that external and sensible objectivity can and must become the real instrument and visible image of divine power ... There is in the Christian Church a materially fixed point, an external and visible centre of action ... the apostolic see of Rome, that miraculous icon of universal Christianity' (V. Soloviev, *Russia and the Universal Church*, ET (London, 1948), p. 16).

17

In his 'systematic global catechesis', which began in December 1984 and is still in progress, Pope John Paul devoted over two years of General Audience addresses to Christology. His intention was to let the form of Christ shine through the mediation of Scripture and Tradition in 'its grandeur and all-embracing nature'.[2] All the false oppositions of the past, from Cerinthus to Bultmann ('the Jesus of history', 'the Christ of faith'), were serenely discarded. The hollowness of modern reductionism, the fashioning of 'a more convenient Jesus' by 'denying His transcendent divinity or dismissing His real, historical humanity', calmly exposed.[3] The vision is Catholic: the Pope strives always to preserve our sense of the *wholeness* of Christ.[4] The figure of Jesus is not cut up into pieces.[5] 'What would be the use of a catechesis on Jesus', asks the Pope, 'if it did not have the authenticity and completeness of view with which the Church contemplates, prays, and announces His mystery?'[6] In the introduction to his Christological discourses, he declared that he would be considering four points:

1) Jesus in His historical reality and in His transcendent messianic character, Son of Abraham, Son of Man and Son of God;

2) Jesus in His identity as true God and true man, in profound communion with the Father and animated by the power of the Holy Spirit as He is presented to us in the Gospel;

3) Jesus as seen by the eyes of the Church, who, with the assistance of the Holy Spirit, has elucidated and investigated the data of revelation by giving us, especially in the Ecumenical Councils, precise formulations of Christological faith;

[2] 7/1/87; *Catechesi* 5, p. 15.
[3] Ibid.
[4] Cf. Rmi 5. See chapter 12 *passim*.
[5] 'It remains incomparable only if the figure of Jesus Christ is not cut to pieces' (Balthasar, *A Short Primer for Unsettled Laymen*, ET (San Francisco, 1985), p. 27).
[6] 7/1/87; *Catechesi* 5, p. 17.

4) finally, Jesus in His life and in His works, Jesus in His redemptive Passion and in His Glorification, Jesus in our midst and within us, in history and in His Church until the end of the world (cf. Matt. 28.20).[7]

Pope John Paul's Christocentricity draws upon the Christology of the Church's Tradition in all its richness – the Scriptures, the Fathers, the Scholastics, the Councils of the Patristic age, the Living Magisterium.[8] The great Ecumenical Councils have been commemorated by Popes in the past, but never before with such enthusiasm. In June 1981, though confined to bed following the attempt on his life the previous month, he supervised the celebration of Constantinople I (381) and Ephesus (431). In 1987, during the Marian Year, he re-stated the Christology of the Second Council of Nicaea (787).[9]

The Holy Father's commitment to expounding the Christology of the first seven Ecumenical Councils is of great ecumenical importance. First, it illustrates once again just how much the Catholic Church shares in common with the Eastern Orthodox Churches, for these councils were celebrated in the East when Rome and Constantinople were still in full communion. They are part of the common patrimony of the first millennium. Secondly, the Pope's Christological mission should have an immediate appeal for Protestant Christians in the West. Conservative Evangelicals are feeling increasingly exasperated with the mainstream Protestant denominations because the latter officially tolerate scepticism about the Divinity, Virginal Conception, and Bodily Resurrection of Christ. It should be of more than a little interest to them to know that it is the very office that claims direct foundation by Jesus (a claim they traditionally reject) which, alone among the leaderships of the Christian bodies of the West, clearly and unambiguously proclaims the Trinitarian and Christological dogmas of Nicaea and the other councils.

---

[7] Ibid., p. 16.
[8] On the great ecumenical councils of the Patristic era, see *Catechesi* 7, pp. 134–157.
[9] On Nicaea II, see *Duodecimum Saeculum*, AAS 80 (1988), 241–252.

4

One of the Trinity

True Christocentricity must be Trinitarian. 'Jesus Christ is indeed the centre of our faith', says Balthasar, 'but only the Christ who is the Father's Son, endowed with the fullness of the Spirit. No Christology without Trinitarian doctrine (and, of course, *vice versa*)'.[1] Pope John Paul has built this axiom into the structure of his teaching. His encyclical on the incarnate Son as 'Redeemer of Man' has been complemented by one on the 'Richly Merciful' Father, whom Christ reveals, and a third on the Holy Spirit, 'the Lord, the Giver of Life', who takes what is Christ's and declares it to us. *Redemptor Hominis*, masterpiece though it is, turns out to be the first panel in a triptych.

The Pope does not forget that Jesus Christ is 'One of the Trinity', God the Son, true God from true God, made true man from the Virgin Mary for our salvation. It is this divine hypostasis who in His humanity has revealed the mystery of mysteries – the Trinitarian inner life of God.[2] As St Maximus the Confessor said, 'theology', that is, the doctrine of the immanent Trinity, is taught us by the incarnate Word Himself, for 'He reveals in Himself the Father and the Holy Spirit'.[3]

In His humanity, as in His divinity, the Son exists 'towards the Father'. He is 'totally directed' to Him, lives for Him, gives the whole of His earthly existence to Him without reserve.[4] Here is the great paradox of this book: Christ Himself is not

[1] *Unser Auftrag*. Bericht und Entwurf (Einsiedeln, 1984), p. 103.
[2] Jesus is the revealer of the Trinity (19/8/87; *Catechesi* 6, pp. 69–73).
[3] *Expositio orationis dominicae*, PG 90. 876C.
[4] 15/7/87, 22/7/87; *Catechesi* 6, pp. 42–52.

Christocentric; His centre is the Father. Against all scepticism about the consciousness of Christ, the Pope asserts that, from His earliest days on earth, Jesus had an awareness in His human mind of the 'unique and exclusive relationship that exists mutually between the Father and Himself'.[5] This is expressed in the name 'Abba' with which He addresses the Father in prayer,[6] a prayer which is always one of gratitude, Eucharist we might even say, because 'at the centre of all that Jesus does and says, there is the awareness of the gift', the gift of His Father.[7] Like Balthasar, the Pope sees the human consciousness of Christ as a 'mission-consciousness', the awareness of being the sent Son.[8]

The incarnate Son is the revealer of the Father, His 'Exegete' (cf. John 1.18). He reveals the Father, and at the same time, as He explains to Peter (cf. Matt. 16.17), the Father reveals Him as Son to men. He reveals the Father 'by manifesting Himself as Son'.[9] This, according to St John, was why the Lord was killed, 'because He not only broke the Sabbath, but also called God His Father, making Himself equal with God' (John 5.18). Pope John Paul adds his own gloss: 'Christ, revealer of the Father and revealer of Himself as Son of the Father, died because until the very end He bore witness to the truth of His divine Sonship'.[10]

The Trinitarian character of the Pope's Christocentricity stands out very clearly in his encyclical on divine mercy, Dives in Misericordia. In the crucified flesh of the Son, in His pierced human heart, Trinitarian love is revealed as mercy, heart-love (misericordia, miserum cor). Christ 'makes [divine mercy] incarnate and personifies it. He Himself, in a certain sense, is mercy'.[11] His mission as Messiah is to 'make the Father present as love and mercy'.[12] The divine Fatherhood is not a concept created by men, a projection of their 'patriarchal' mentality, but

[5] 1/7/87; Catechesi 6, p. 33.
[6] 1/7/87, 22/7/87; Catechesi 6, pp. 35, 47–52.
[7] 29/7/87; Catechesi 6, pp. 35, 47–52.
[8] Cf. Balthasar, TD 2/2, pp. 149–185.
[9] 30/10/85.
[10] Ibid.
[11] DM 2; AAS 72 (1980), 1180.
[12] Ibid., 3, 1184.

a reality revealed by the only-begotten Son, and the reality is merciful love. God the Father so loves the world that He gives it His Son (cf. John 3.16). The Father's 'philanthropy' is prodigally, foolishly generous. As the character Adam in Wojtyla's play, *Radiation of Fatherhood*, says:

> Love reveals the Father in the Son. How much He strives for every human being – as for the greatest treasure, as someone in love strives for his beloved.[13]

A Pneumatological Christocentricity

Pope John Paul's Christocentricity is fully Trinitarian, not merely binitarian. He contemplates Christ in His filial relationship to the Father *in the Holy Spirit*. In fact it may even be called a Pneumatological Christocentricity. Jesus is *ho Christos*, 'the one anointed with the Holy Spirit'.[14] In His human nature, from the first moment of His conception, the eternal Son 'receives from the Holy Spirit an extraordinary fullness of holiness, in a measure corresponding to the dignity of His divine Person'.[15] From conception to Cross, Jesus lives out the mission given Him by the Father 'in the power of the Holy Spirit'.[16] A 'Pneumatological integration with Christology – as the Orientals observe – seems to be inevitable'.[17] This means 'following the action of the Holy Spirit in the life and mission of Christ: in His childhood, in the inauguration of His public life through His Baptism, in His sojourn in the desert, in prayer, in preaching, in Sacrifice, and finally in Resurrection'.[18]

Pope John Paul devoted a large part of his encyclical *Dominum et Vivificantem*, as well as several of his catechetical addresses, to meditation on the Holy Spirit's role in the Virginal Conception of Christ. Taking up a theme that we find in St Augustine and St Thomas, he points out how appropriate it is that the supreme manifestation of the Trinity's love of mankind,

[13] Karol Wojtyla, *The Collected Plays and Writings on Theater* (Berkeley, 1987), p. 362.
[14] DV 15; AAS 78 (1986), 822.
[15] 6/6/90.
[16] 5/8/87; *Catechesi* 6, p. 58.
[17] 28/3/90.
[18] Ibid.

the Incarnation of the Son, should take place in the Virgin's womb by the power of the Holy Spirit, the 'Person–Love', the 'Person–Gift':

> The conception and birth of Jesus Christ are in fact the greatest work accomplished by the Holy Spirit in the history of creation and salvation; the supreme grace – 'the grace of union', source of every other grace, as St Thomas explains.[19]

To effect the Incarnation, the Holy Spirit worked on both the virginal body and the spotless soul of Mary. 'The Holy Spirit sees to it that Mary is perfectly prepared to become the Mother of God's Son, and that, in view of this divine motherhood, she is and remains a virgin.'[20] Our Lady's Yes is 'a fruit of the power of the Holy Spirit', who has filled her heart since her Immaculate Conception. 'It is an answer given *by* grace and *in* grace, which comes from the Holy Spirit.'[21] At the same time it is an act of Mary's human free will. The Holy Spirit acts inwardly upon her response to ensure it is 'precisely what it ought to be', an act of 'mature love', the perfect example of the human person's response to God.[22]

One of the most original features of the Holy Father's Christology is his understanding of the Holy Spirit's role in the Sacrifice of the Incarnate Son.[23] He unfolds a text in the Epistle to the Hebrews which speaks of Christ offering Himself to God 'through the eternal Spirit' (cf. Heb. 9.13f.). In His Passion, from Gethsemane to Golgotha, Christ, 'in His own humanity opened Himself totally to [the] action of the Spirit-Paraclete, who from suffering enables eternal salvific love to spring forth'.[24] In 'the ardent prayer of His Passion', Christ enabled the Spirit to transform His humanity 'into a perfect sacrifice through the act of His death as the victim of love on the Cross'.[25] Only the Second Person of the Blessed Trinity suffers on the Cross in His humanity. Nonetheless, the Holy Spirit is also at work in the

---

[19] DV 50, 870.
[20] 4/4/90.
[21] 18/4/90.
[22] Ibid.
[23] Cf. DV 40f., 854ff.
[24] Ibid., 855.
[25] Ibid.

Sacrifice of the Son, 'bringing it into the divine reality of the Trinitarian communion'.[26] In the language of the Bible, He 'consumes' the Sacrifice with the fire of the love uniting Father and Son in the communion of the Trinity.[27] Within the Godhead the Son loves the Father, and the Father loves the Son, in the Spirit. In His manhood, too, with His human heart, the Son lovingly obeys the Father 'in the Spirit', in perfect docility to the Spirit's promptings. Thus Christ offered Himself on the Cross ' through the eternal Spirit'. As St Thomas says, 'by the motion and impulse of the Holy Spirit, that is, through love of God and neighbour, Christ did this'.[28] Moreover, the Spirit who played this part in the Sacrifice of the Son on Calvary is also at work in its sacramental representation on the altars of the Church, as several prayers of the liturgy attest.[29]

If John Paul's Christocentricity is Pneumatological, his Pneumatology is Christocentric. The Holy Spirit is, as St Cyril of Alexandria insisted against Nestorius, Christ's 'own' Holy Spirit, the Spirit of God, but also the Spirit of Jesus.[30] He is the Spirit of the Father and the Son, proceeding from Father and Son as from one principle.[31] He is sent from the Father by the incarnate, crucified, and risen Son to complete His work on earth, 'to transform us', as the Pope says quoting St Cyril, 'into His own risen image'.[32] He is the gift of the glorified Christ. In a beautiful passage of *Dominum et Vivificantem*, the Pope says that the risen Christ gives the disciples the Spirit 'as it were through the wounds of His Crucifixion'.[33] The Holy Spirit 'comes after Him and because of Him', 'at the price' of Christ's 'departure'.[34] The divine missions of the Son and the Spirit are intimately linked: there is no sending of the Spirit without the Cross and

[26] Ibid., 41, 856.
[27] Ibid.
[28] St Thomas Aquinas, *In Epistolam ad Hebraeos*, cap. 9, lectio 4.
[29] Cf. DV 41, 857.
[30] Cf. *Adversus Nestorium* 4, 1; PG 76. 172f.
[31] Cf. DV 14, 821.
[32] DV 24, 832.
[33] Ibid.
[34] Ibid., 3, 813.

Resurrection of the incarnate Son, but the redemptive mission was carried out by the Son in the power of the Spirit and is now continued in human hearts and minds by 'the Other Counsellor'.[35]

It is the Holy Spirit who keeps the Church Christocentric, centred on the Word made flesh. He is not a Spirit of disincarnation. He never takes us away from, but only ever more deeply into, the flesh-and-blood reality of Jesus. That is why the Eucharistic epiclesis is a paradigm for understanding His work. It is the Paraclete who ensures that the truth the Apostles heard from their Master lives on in the Church.[36] He guides them and their successors into all the truth (John 16.12f.).[37] In the teaching and Sacraments of the Church, He 'unceasingly continues the historical presence on earth of the Redeemer and His saving work'.[38] The Spirit, 'the soul of the Mystical Body', furnishes and directs the Church with His gifts, both hierarchical and charismatic, and so leads the Bride into ever more perfect union with the Bridegroom.[39]

[35] Ibid., 24, 832f.
[36] Ibid., 4 & 5, 814f.
[37] Ibid., 6, 815f.
[38] Ibid., 7, 816.
[39] Ibid., 25, 835, quoting LG 25.

5

The Christocentric Mary

The Christocentric Mary

The Blessed Virgin is the very air the Pope breathes. From the first moment of his pontificate he has declared himself to be totally hers.[1] His teaching is Christocentric not despite or in addition to this Marian dedication, but because of it. Mary is the supremely Christ-centred person, and the surest way for every person to true Christ-centredness. Her whole mission is to bring Christ to men and men to Christ. For this she was predestined and created, for this she was engraced from her conception. To go to Jesus through Mary, therefore, is to take the most direct route, the straightest and swiftest path:

> No one in the history of the world has been more Christocentric and Christophoric than she. And no one has been more like Him, not only with the natural likeness of mother and son, but with the likeness of the Spirit and holiness.[2]

On earth Our Lady loved and served Jesus with an immaculate heart, with the dedication of her whole personality, and in Heaven she still co-operates with Him. By her motherly

---

[1] On the Montfortian inspiration of the Holy Father's consecration to Christ through the hands of Mary (cf. RM 48), see Alphonse Bossard SMM, 'L'encyclique *Redemptoris Mater* et Saint Louis-Marie de Montfort', *Marianum* 139 (1989), 261–268. The formula *totus tuus* is Christocentric in the way it is expressed by St Louis de Montfort: 'I am all yours, and all I have is yours, O dear Jesus, through Mary, your holy Mother' (*True Devotion to the Blessed Virgin*, n. 233 in *God Alone: The Collected Writings of St Louis Marie de Montfort*, ET (Bay Shore, 1987), p. 364).

[2] St Mary Major, 8/12/80.

intercession, she summons us unceasingly to the Son and so to the Father in the Holy Spirit:

> It was because she received the Word of God both in her heart and in her body that the Blessed Virgin has a unique role in the mystery of the Word Incarnate and in that of the Mystical Body. She is closely united with the Church, for which she is the model of faith, charity, and perfect union with Christ. In this way, in answer to our devotion and our prayer, Mary, who in a way gathers and reflects in herself the highest aspirations of faith, calls the faithful to the Son and to His Sacrifice, as well as to the love of the Father.[3]

The Son of God is inseparable from the woman in whose flesh and by whose faith He became man.[4] Pope John Paul has reaffirmed this indissoluble bond by actions as well as words. In 1983 it was indicated by the Pope's decision to open the Jubilee of the Redemption on the Solemnity of the Annunciation, the day when 'Mary of Nazareth ... accepts into her womb and into her heart the Son of God as the Son of Man'.[5] Similarly, from Pentecost 1987 to the Assumption 1988, the third millennium of the Incarnation of the Son was prepared for by an 'Advent' year devoted to the Mother.

The Pope's Christocentricity is Marian, and his Mariology is Christocentric. He looks on Jesus through Mary, but he looks on Mary through Jesus.[6] With the Fathers of the Second Vatican Council, he contemplates 'the Blessed Virgin Mary, the Mother of God' not in isolation, but 'in the mystery of Christ and the Church'.[7] In the first part of *Redemptoris Mater*, he takes a text from *Gaudium et Spes* concerned with the Christocentricity of Christian anthropology and transforms it into an axiom for Mariology:

> If it is true, as the Council itself proclaims, that 'only in the mystery of the Incarnate Word does the mystery of man take on light', then this principle must be applied in a very particular way

[3] To Dutch Bishops, 31/1/80.
[4] 10/12/88, cf. LG 53.
[5] 25/3/83.
[6] Cf. RM 26, 396.
[7] LG cap. 8.

to that exceptional 'daughter of the human race', that extraordinary woman who became the Mother of Christ. Only in the mystery of Christ is her mystery fully clear.[8]

Here, says Balthasar, the Pope demonstrates clearly that 'the whole of Mariology belongs within Christology and can only be justified and made comprehensible by Christology'.[9] No Christology without Mariology, no Mariology without Christology.

Mother of God

Everything in Mary has a reference to Christ. As the Fathers teach, from St Cyril of Alexandria to St John Damascene, the very name 'Theotokos' is a compendium of the Church's faith in the Incarnation. In the words of Damascene:

This name expresses the whole mystery of the economy. If she who gave birth is Mother of God, then He who was born of her is definitely God and also definitely man . . . This [name] signifies the one hypostasis and the two natures and the two births of Our Lord Jesus Christ.[10]

In his addresses during the 1981 commemoration of the Council of Ephesus, and then in his great encyclicals for the Marian Year, *Redemptoris Mater* and *Mulieris Dignitatem*, the Holy Father has continued this Patristic teaching:

Mary is the Mother of God (= *Theotokos*), since by the operation of the Holy Spirit she conceived in her virginal womb and gave to the world Jesus Christ, the Son of God consubstantial with the Father. 'The Son of God . . . born of the Virgin Mary . . . has truly been made one of us', has been made man. Thus, through the mystery of Christ, on the horizon of the Church's faith there

---

[8] RM 4, 364. In *Crossing the Threshold of Hope*, the Pope says that it was 'thanks to St Louis of Montfort' that he 'came to understand that true devotion to the Mother of God is actually Christocentric, indeed, it is very profoundly rooted in the Mystery of the Blessed Trinity, and the mysteries of the Incarnation and Redemption' ((New York, 1994), p. 213).

[9] Balthasar, *Maria*, p. 131.

[10] *De Fide Orthodoxa* 3, 12; PG 94. 1029CD. Cf. St Cyril: 'To confess our faith in orthodox fashion . . . it is enough to confess that the Blessed Virgin is Theotokos' (*Homiliae Diversae* 15; PG 77. 1093C).

shines the mystery of His Mother. The dogma of Mary's divine motherhood was for the Council of Ephesus and is for the Church like a confirmation (*quasi fidem fecit*) of the dogma of the Incarnation, in which the Word truly assumes human nature into the unity of His person, without cancelling out that nature.[11]

The words used here to describe the divine motherhood – *quasi fidem fecit*, 'like a confirmation' or, as the Vatican Press translation has it 'like a seal' – are reminiscent of Cardinal Newman's in his discourse on 'The Glories of Mary for the Sake of her Son':

> The confession that Mary is *Deipara*, or the Mother of God, is that safeguard wherewith we seal up and secure the doctrine of the Apostles from all evasion, and that test whereby we detect all the pretences of those bad spirits of 'Antichrist which have gone out into the world'. It declares that He is God; it implies that He is man; it suggests to us that He is God still, though He has become man, and that He is true man though He is God.[12]

More briefly, as the Pope says, Mary is 'almost the identity-card for the truth of the Incarnation'.[13] She is not only the guarantee but the living embodiment of orthodox faith in Christ and the Trinity.[14]

In his unfolding of Our Lady's divine motherhood the Holy Father builds upon the insights of his philosophical anthropology. The personalism of his Lublin Thomism gives him a heightened sensitivity to the Patristic distinction between person (or hypostasis) and nature:

> Of the essence of motherhood is the fact that it concerns the person. Motherhood always establishes a unique and unrepeatable relationship between two people; between mother and child, and between child and mother.[15]

The Orthodox theologian Bishop Kallistos Ware has suggested that the Pope's Mariological personalism is in continuity

---

[11] RM 4, 365.

[12] 'The Glories of Mary for the Sake of her Son', *Discourses Addressed to Mixed Congregations*, new ed. (London & New York, 1892), p. 347f.

[13] 4/4/90.

[14] In the words of the ancient antiphon, the Mother of God is 'victorious over all heresies'.

[15] RM 45, 422.

with that of St Cyril of Alexandria.[16] Despite the limitations of his technical vocabulary, St Cyril was able to show, against Nestorius, that the name 'Theotokos' does not imply that the Holy Virgin gave birth to the divine nature. It is not natures, but persons-in-nature, that are born of mothers. Mary is rightly and properly called 'Mother of God', because the person to whom she gives birth is a divine person, the Second Person of the Blessed Trinity, but it is of course in His human nature, not His divine nature, that He is born of her. The very same person who in His divinity is eternally begotten of God the Father without a mother is born in His humanity of the Virgin Mother without a Father.[17]

Mother of the Whole Christ

It would be foolish to oppose or even contrast 'Christ-centred' and 'Church-centred' Mariologies, for the Virgin's Son is inseparable from His Church. Pope John Paul, like the Fathers of the Second Vatican Council, sees the Theotokos united by a 'twofold bond' with Christ and His Church.[18] She is the Church's supreme 'model' and 'constant point of reference' in 'faith, charity, and perfect union with Christ'.[19] But that is not all: the model is also mother. Those who strive to imitate Mary are her children and loved by her. Thus 'the Church's motherhood is accomplished not only according to the model and figure of the Mother of God, but also with her co-operation'.[20] By her intercession Mary mothers the Church into mothering. She is Mother of the Church; in a certain sense, she *is* Mother Church.[21] She is the Church's most perfect image, her beginning and first flowering, 'first Church', *Kirche im Ursprung*, as

[16] Cf. 'Mary Theotokos in the Orthodox Tradition', *Marianum* 140 (1990), 215.
[17] See my article 'The Theotokos in the Theology of the Church', *Chrysostom* 6 (1984), 205–233.
[18] Cf. RM 5, 366.
[19] Cf. LG 63, cited in RM 5, 366.
[20] RM 44, 421. At the Council, in a written *animadversio* on chapter 8 of the ecclesiological schema, Archbishop Wojtyla wrote: 'This mother hood of the Church exists first and foremost in the hands and heart of the Most Blessed Virgin, and is intimately linked with the office of Mediatrix' (*Acta Synodalia Sacrosancti Concilii Oecumenici Vaticani II I/4* (Vatican City, 1971), p. 598).
[21] Cf. Balthasar in *Maria*, p. 138f.

Balthasar and Ratzinger so finely say.[22] All that the Church hopes to be in Christ, she already is.[23] The Bride's final beautification is not a dream, but even now, in Mary, a glorious reality.

Christocentric Virginity

Whatever the Triune Mary bestows upon Mary, whatever she by His grace says and does, is for the sake of Christ and His Church. It is therefore for Him that she is ever-virgin. It is because of who her Son is, the eternal consubstantial Son of the Father, that by the power of the Holy Spirit she conceives Him without seed and gives birth to Him without corruption. It is for Him that she dedicates her whole self, in body and in soul, to remain a virgin for ever.

In 1992, on the sixteenth centenary of the Council of Capua, the Holy Father gave an immensely rich and detailed exposition of 'the virginity of Christ's humble and glorious Mother'.[24] It is, said the Pope, 'a "Christological theme" before being a "Mariological question"'. This was recognized by the Church Fathers, who 'observed that the virginity of the Mother is a requirement flowing from the divine nature of the Son'. For the Christian Tradition, Our Lady's virginal womb, made fruitful by the Holy Spirit without human intervention, becomes, like the wood of the Cross or the wrappings in the empty tomb, 'a reason and sign for recognizing in Jesus of Nazareth the Son of God'.[25] The Pope had already presented the following classical argument for the fittingness of the Virginal Conception in one of his Christological catecheses:

> The fact that Jesus did not have an earthly father because generated 'without human intervention' sets out clearly the truth that He is the Son of God, so much so that even when He assumes human nature His Father remains exclusively God.[26]

---

[22] Balthasar & Ratzinger, *Maria – Kirche im Ursprung* (Freiburg, Basle & Vienna, 1986).
[23] Cf. LG 65; RM 6, 367.
[24] *L'Osservatore Romano* (10 June 1992), 13ff.
[25] Ibid.
[26] 28/1/87, *Catechesi* 5, 27f.

Through the wonder of the Virginal Conception, Christ continues to be, even in His humanity, 'the Son of the same Father of whom He is eternally begotten' in His divinity.[27]

In Capua the Holy Father vigorously reaffirmed the traditional doctrine of Our Lady's virginity *in partu*. He offered beautiful insights into the truth taught by the Second Vatican Council when it said that in His birth Mary's Son 'did not diminish her virginal integrity but sanctified it'.[28] Following the Fathers, the Pope points to the important link between the beginning and end of Christ's earthly life: just as He was born of an 'intact Virgin' so He rises from an 'intact tomb'. He quotes St Peter Chrysologus:

> Him whom *clausa virginitas* had brought to this life, the *clausum sepulcrum* would return to eternal life. It is characteristic of divinity to leave the Virgin sealed after birth; it is also characteristic of divinity to go out from the sealed tomb with the body.[29]

Incarnation is not invasion. In becoming man, the Son of God neither abandons His divinity nor absorbs our humanity. The uniting of man's nature to God's in the person of the Word is an act of infinite delicacy: it takes place 'without separation or division, without confusion or change'. So precious is our humanity to the assuming Word that He does not abolish or diminish it. He comes to beautify not destroy, to raise up, not to crush. The Father's Word and Wisdom 'orders all things sweetly' (cf. Wisd. 8.1). That is why, in taking flesh from the Virgin, He does not merely employ her as a passive instrument, but, with a kind of divine courtesy,[30] asks for and makes possible her active consent. And as He enters Mary's womb, so He leaves it – without hurt or harm of its maidenly wholeness. In the way He is conceived and born, God the Son shows He is faithful to His own commandment: He *honours* His Mother.

[27] 28/5/90.
[28] LG 57.
[29] *Sermo* 75, 3; CCSL 24A. 460.
[30] The word and concept of courtesy comes from the Christian culture of the Middle Ages. It is frequently found in Dante, and re-appears in the medieval English mystics. Hilaire Belloc has sung the praises of this forgotten virtue: 'The first was of Saint Gabriel;/On wings a-flame from heaven he fell;/And as he went upon one knee/He shone with Heavenly Courtesy' (*Sonnets and Verse* (London, 1923), p. 51).

When discussing the Virgin Birth, the Pope explains how the Church loves to tread the path that leads from the Cross back to the Crib. She celebrates Christmas with an eye on Easter, but she does not forget Christmas at Easter. She 'recognizes in Mary the exceptional witness to the identity of the Child born of her virginal flesh and the Crucified One, reborn from the sealed tomb'.[31] The Virginal Conception and Birth of Jesus, on the one hand, and His Bodily Resurrection, on the other, stand or fall together because of their intimate connection with faith in Jesus' divinity:

> History shows that doubts or uncertainty about one has inevitable repercussions on the other, just as, on the contrary, humble and strong assent to one of them fosters the warm acceptance of the other.[32]

Our Lady is virgin not only before and during, but also for ever after, the birth of Jesus. She is *aeiparthenos*, 'Ever-Virgin'. This life-long virginity is likewise Christocentric and theocentric. Mary's consent to divine motherhood springs from 'her total self-giving to God in virginity':

> Mary accepted her election as Mother of the Son of God, guided by spousal love, the love which totally 'consecrates' a human being to God. By virtue of this love, Mary wished to be always and in all things 'given to God' (*Deo donata*), living in virginity. The words 'Behold the handmaid of the Lord' express the fact that from the outset she accepted and understood her own motherhood as a total gift of self, a gift of her person to the service of the saving plans of the Most High. And to the very end she lived her entire maternal sharing in the life of Jesus Christ, her Son, in a way that matched her vocation to virginity.[33]

The Holy Father clearly shows that the virginity of Our Lady is not some minor detail, but a kind of summary, of the whole of Divine Revelation. The more a man meditates upon it, the more he 'comes into contact, so to speak, with the whole of

---

[31] 24/5/92.

[32] Ibid.

[33] RM 39, 412f. Pope John Paul also explicitly re-stated the teaching of the Council of the Lateran (649) on Our Lady's perpetual virginity in the Christological Catecheses (28/2/87; *Catechesi* 5, p. 25; cf. DS 503).

Scripture'. In the formation of Adam from the 'virgin earth' (cf. Gen. 2.4B-7), and then in all the examples of undamaged integrity in the Old Covenant (the Burning Bush, the Closed Door of the Temple, the Stone Uncut by Human Hand), we have the preparations and promises of the Virgin Theotokos. All the graces given to the Patriarchs lead up to the astonishing plenitude of grace given, even from her conception, to this lowly maiden of Israel. All the blessings showered on Mary have this one end: to enable her, in the whole of her being and at every moment of her life, to dedicate herself to the Son of God:

> From the moment of the Annunciation, Mary knew that she was to fulfil her virginal desire to give herself exclusively and fully to God precisely by becoming the Mother of God's Son. Becoming a Mother by the power of the Holy Spirit was the form taken by her gift of self: a form which God Himself expected of the Virgin Mary, who was 'betrothed' to Joseph.[34]

Immaculate Conception and Assumption

The Immaculate Conception is a Christocentric mystery. Its final cause is Our Lady's mothering of God-made-man: she is immaculately conceived in order to prepare her to be Theotokos. Its meritorious cause is Christ's Sacrifice on Calvary: it is by the power of Christ's redeeming death that Mary is preserved from all stain of Original Sin:

> By virtue of the richness of the grace of the beloved Son, by reason of the redemptive merits of Him who willed to become her Son, Mary was preserved from the inheritance of Original Sin. In this way, from the first moment of her conception – which is to say of her existence – she belonged to Christ, sharing in salvific and sanctifying grace and in that love which has its beginning in the 'Beloved', the Son of the Father, who through the Incarnation became her own Son.[35]

It is the Immaculate Conception which makes Mary so perfectly Christocentric. Through this 'pre-redemption', the divine Redeemer centres His Mother totally on Himself from the beginning of her existence, so that she may love Him with a

[34] *Redemptoris Custos*, n. 17.
[35] RM 10, 322.

spotless, undivided heart. That is why she is the safest guide towards Christ-centredness and Christ-likeness. Pope John Paul explains that, in turning to Christ, he unites himself with Mary, because 'nobody else can bring us as Mary can into the divine and human dimension of [the mystery of Redemption]. Nobody has been brought into it by God Himself as Mary has'.[36] The active Christ-centredness of Mary's faith and intercession depends on the passive Christ-centredness of her election and engracing.[37]

The bodily Assumption of Our Lady also has a Christocentric meaning. Mary is the first to share in her Son's victory over death in body as well as soul, because she 'belongs' to Christ, is 'of Christ' (cf. 1 Cor. 15.20–23), in a unique way.[38] This dogmatic truth means, as Balthasar says in his commentary on *Redemptoris Mater*, that Mary's mothering of the Church is not purely spiritual: there is 'something supremely bodily and real, something historical' about it.[39] The special powers of presence enjoyed by the risen body – what the Scholastics call its 'agility', its ability to obey the soul with supreme swiftness of movement – are employed in Mary's motherhood in the order of grace. In her glorified flesh she enjoys a homely intimacy with her children in their mortal flesh. The faithful sense this with particular keenness, says the Pope, at Jasna Gora, Lourdes, Fatima, and the other Marian sanctuaries and shrines.[40]

The Faith of the Christocentric Mary

Mary's Christocentricity engages her whole person. Faith and flesh are inseparable; what is spiritual is also bodily, what is bodily is spiritual. As Pope St Leo the Great taught, following St Augustine, the Blessed Virgin conceived the Word in her mind in faith before conceiving Him in her womb in

[36] RH 22, 322.
[37] Cf. RM 9–10, 371f.
[38] 15/8/80.
[39] Balthasar, *Maria*, p. 139.
[40] 'In all these places that unique testament of the Crucified Lord is wonderfully actualized. In them man feels that he is entrusted and confided to Mary. He goes there in order to be with her, as with his Mother. He opens his heart to her and speaks to her about everything' (Fatima, 13/5/82).

flesh.[41] Leo's successor, John Paul II, expressed the same truth by saying that Mary accepts 'into her womb and into her heart' the Son of God as Son of Man.[42]

Redemptoris Mater is the most detailed papal exposition of Our Lady's faith in the history of the Church. In fact, in Balthasar's opinion, no other Mariology has placed Mary's faith so centrally and with such deliberation.[43] Certain of its more original features deserve to be mentioned here. First, the Holy Father throws Marian light on the teaching of Vatican I and Vatican II on revelation and faith. Mary at the Annunciation entrusts herself wholeheartedly to God, with the 'full submission of intellect and will', co-operating perfectly with 'the grace of God that precedes and assists'.[44] Secondly, the Pope notes that Mary says Yes to God with 'her whole human and feminine person' (*tota sua persona humana, feminea*).[45] This is later developed in *Mulieris Dignitatem*. The model for the soul of every Christian man and woman in relation to God is a woman, the Virgin Mother Mary. Thirdly, the Pope sketches the historical 'journey' of Our Lady's faith from the moment of the Incarnation onwards: the nine months when God Incarnate is quite literally 'central' to her,[46] the birth in Bethlehem, the Presentation in the Temple, the Flight into Egypt, the humble life in Nazareth when 'Mary's life too is "hid with Christ in God" (cf. Col. 3.3)',[47] finally the vigil at the foot of the Cross, where her faith enters the night. On Golgotha Mary is united with Jesus in His self-emptying, 'the deepest "kenosis" of faith in human history'.[48] In this costliest moment of her faith, we have the model and the beginning of the Church's co-operation with her Head. Here begins her Eucharistic attitude, here her mysticism, here her mission of compassion.

[41] RM 13, 376.
[42] 25/3/83.
[43] *Maria*, p. 133.
[44] Cf. RM 13, 375; cf. DS 3008, 3010.
[45] Ibid.
[46] 'The Son's mission begins in her, under her heart' (3/12/79). See my book *Redeemer in the Womb*. Jesus Living in Mary (San Francisco, 1993).
[47] RM 17, 380.
[48] RM 18, 383.

Mary's Motherly Mediation of Grace

Everything in Christ is for participation. Head and members are like 'one mystical person',[49] and so whatever He is or has in His human nature is, in a certain way, for them to share. He is the true and natural son of God; through our incorporation into Him we become sons of God by grace and adoption, sons-in-the-Son. He suffered once for all for our sins on the Cross, yet we can share His suffering, 'completing what is lacking in His afflictions for the sake of His Body, that is, the Church' (Col. 1.24). In and through His superabundant satisfaction we make satisfaction.[50] *Lumen Gentium* applies this theology of the Whole Christ – the doctrine of Paul, Augustine, Thomas and Trent – to Our Lady's mediation of grace:

> No creature could ever be classed with the Incarnate Word and Redeemer. But just as the priesthood of Christ is shared in various ways both by sacred ministers and by His faithful, and as the one goodness of God is in reality communicated diversely to His creatures, so also the unique mediation of the Redeemer does not exclude but rather gives rise among creatures to a manifold co-operation, which is but sharing in this unique source.[51]

In *Redemptoris Mater* Pope John Paul examines this statement more deeply and 'gives it a new weight for theology and religious piety'. He expounds Our Lady's mediation theologically, says Cardinal Ratzinger, 'while safeguarding it from all danger of misunderstanding'.[52] In so doing, he reveals the true meaning of Catholic Christocentricity. Christ's mediation is utterly unique (cf. 1 Tim. 2.5–6). No one can rival Him as mediator between God and man, for He alone is true God and true man in one person. However, this mediatorial uniqueness is inclusive, not exclusive; it makes participation possible. Cardinal Ratzinger explains as follows:

[49] Cf. St Thomas, ST 3a 48, 2, ad 1.

[50] Cf. The Council of Trent, 14th Session, Doctrine on the Sacrament of Penance (1551), chapter 8, DS 1690–1692.

[51] LG 62; *Decreta*, p. 200. See Salvatore M. Meo OSM, 'La "mediazione materna" di Maria nell' enciclica *Redemptoris Mater*' (*Marianum* 139 (1989), 145–170).

[52] Ratzinger, *Maria*, p. 120.

The uniqueness of Christ does not extinguish the actuality and co-operation of human beings among themselves before God. In many different ways, one for another, they can all be mediators with God in communion with Jesus Christ. This is a simple fact of our daily experience. No one believes on his own. Each person lives his faith thanks to human mediations. None of these would be sufficient to make a bridge to God, because no human being of himself can give an absolute guarantee of God's existence and nearness. However, in communion with Him who is this nearness in His very person, human beings can be and are such mediators.[53]

The spiritual give-and-take in the Mystical Body is what Catholic Tradition calls the *Communio Sanctorum*. By the power of the Head, grace flows from Him to His members and then among the members themselves. St Paul describes the rippling flood at the beginning of his Second Letter to the Corinthians. Whatever he receives from God in Christ, he says, be it comfort or affliction, is for the salvation of others (cf. 2. Cor. 1.3–6). Through the grace of our Head we are sons-in-the-Son, and therefore also 'mediators-in-the-Mediator'.

Our Lady's mediation resembles this mediation among Christ's member. It too is 'participated', a 'subordinate role' (*munus subordinatum*),[54] the work of the supremely humble Handmaid of the Lord. It 'flows from the superabundance of the merits of Christ, is founded on His mediation, absolutely depends on it, and draws all its efficacy from it'.[55] However, though it shares these essential characteristics with the other participations in the Mystical Body, the mediating role of the Theotokos, like her person, is 'special and extraordinary' (*peculiare et extraordinarium*).[56] It surpasses all the other sharings and reciprocities in the Communion of Saints.

What is special about Mary's mediation is what is special about her: it is motherly, the mediation of the woman who is God's mother and ours. 'It flows from her divine motherhood and can be understood and lived in faith only on

[53] Ibid., p. 121.
[54] LG 62; *Decreta*, p. 200.
[55] LG 60 cited in RM 38, 411.
[56] RM 38, 412.

the basis of the full truth of this motherhood.' Her first and most fundamental act of mediation is her divine motherhood. Corporeally and spiritually, she mediates the Mediator with a faith and love both virginal and spousal, she brings the eternal Son into the world, welcomes Him into human nature. At every stage of His earthly mission, from His conception in her womb to His death on the Cross, she is His handmaiden and co-operator, an 'associate of unique nobility', completely open to His person and saving work, and so to us, His brethren and hers. Finally, on Calvary, 'she unites herself with a maternal heart to His Sacrifice, and lovingly consents to the immolation of this Victim which she herself had brought forth':[57]

> Along the path of this collaboration with the work of her Son, the Redeemer, Mary's motherhood itself underwent a singular transformation, becoming ever more imbued with 'burning charity' towards all those to whom Christ's mission was directed. Through this 'burning charity', which sought to achieve, in union with Christ, the restoration of 'supernatural life to souls', Mary entered, in a way all her own, into the mediation 'between God and men' which is the mediation of the man Christ Jesus.[58]

Our Lady's enlarged spiritual motherhood comes into its own after her Son's Ascension. When He sends the Holy Spirit upon her and the Apostles at Pentecost, '[Mary's] motherhood remains in the Church as maternal mediation: interceding for all her children, the Mother co-operates in the saving work of her Son, the Redeemer of the world'.[59] As the Council teaches, her motherhood 'in the order of grace' lasts for ever 'until the eternal fulfilment of all the elect'. She has not laid aside her saving role. Glorified in body and soul, 'by her manifold acts of intercession [she] continues to win for us the gifts of eternal salvation'.[60]

As Mediatrix, Mary in no sense 'gets in the way' between Christ and us. By grace she is utterly transparent to grace. In her no sinful self blocks the streams that run from His heart. In

[57] LG 58 cited in RM 18, 382.
[58] RM 39, 413f.
[59] RM 40, 415.
[60] LG 62 cited in RM 40, 415.

the words of Gerard Manley Hopkins, she lets 'all God's glory through'.[61] In the lights of the Immaculate Conception we can say that it is Christ the Mediator Himself who prepares His Mother to be such a selfless Mediatrix:

> Through this fullness of grace and supernatural life she was especially predisposed to co-operation with Christ, the one Mediator of human salvation, and such co-operation is precisely this mediation subordinated to the mediation of Christ.[62]

The great originality of *Redemptor Mater* is that its theology of Marian mediation takes up not only the obviously relevant episodes in St John's Gospel (Cana, the Foot of the Cross), but also what Cardinal Ratzinger has called the apparently 'anti-Marian' texts in St Luke's Gospel (cf. Luke 8.21; 11.28). These words, in which, on a superficial reading, Our Lord might seem to be distancing Himself from His Mother, in fact reveal her true glory:

> [St Luke] shows that Mary's Motherhood is nor merely a unique and unrepeatable biological event, but that she was mother with her whole person and therefore she remains such still.[63]

Thanks for the Feminine
The Marian Christocentricity of Pope John Paul II has bequeathed the Church, first in *Redemptoris Mater* and later in *Mulieris Dignitatem*, a rich theology of womanhood.[64] He shares the Patristic and medieval perception that the restoration of humanity, like its downfall, was the work of a man and a woman.[65] From Genesis to the Apocalypse the male Saviour is linked with 'the Woman', New Adam with New Eve.[66] She is foreshadowed in the promise made to our exiled first parents,

---

[61] 'The Blessed Virgin compared to the Air we Breathe', *The Poems of Gerard Manley Hopkins*, 4th ed. (London, 1970), p. 95.

[62] RM 39, 414.

[63] Ratzinger, *Maria*, p. 123.

[64] See also CL, 49–52; AAS 81 (1989), 486–498.

[65] 'One man and one woman did us grievous harm, but thanks be to God, by another man and another woman everything is restored to us' (St Bernard of Clairvaux, *Dominica infra octavam Assumptionis, Sermo; Sanctis Bernardi Opera* (Rome, 1968), p. 262).

[66] RM 47, 426.

and she shines ahead of us, the glorious embodiment of our hopes. She stands at the centre of history's centre (the Incarnation of God), sharing fully in it 'with her personal and feminine I'. When God asks mankind for an answer of faith, it is a maiden not a man who speaks. To adapt something Chesterton said, men are men, but in humanity's finest hour, man is a woman.[67] She is, therefore, 'the "new beginning" of the dignity and vocation of women, of each and every woman'.[68]

The woman in and through whom the Incarnation takes place enjoys 'a union with God that exceeds all the expectations of the human spirit'.[69] The highest elevation of human nature took place in the masculine gender, when the divine person of the Son of God became man and male. But the highest elevation of the human person took place in the feminine gender, in Mary, the Virgin Mother of God. The greatest after God is a woman.[70] The only truly fulfilled human person, the person already glorified in body as well as soul, is not a male but a female – the Lord's lowly handmaid, the incandescent Queen of Heaven.

Since grace fulfils nature, does not destroy it, we can say, we must say, that the fullness of grace given to the Theotokos is the perfection of femininity.[71] The wonderful coincidence in her of virginity and motherhood, far from making her remote from other women, makes her accessible as a model to women in every state of life. Mary, Virgin and Mother, discloses to us that attitude of receptivity which is quintessentially feminine but also the proper disposition of the creature, whether man or woman, in relation to God. In the light of the Mother of God we see all womanhood, all creatureliness, anew.

John Paul II's Marian theology of womanhood has many strong affinities with the thinking of Balthasar. Indeed, the Pope quotes him in a footnote in *Mulieris Dignitatem*. There is no doubt that the Pope would endorse the Swiss theologian's warning in *Elucidations*:

[67] Cf. *The Napoleon of Notting Hill*, new ed. (London, 1928), p. 14.
[68] MD 3, 1659.
[69] MD 3, 1659.
[70] Cf. M. J. Scheeben, *Handbuch der katholischen Dogmatik*, vol. 2, new ed. (Freiburg, 1933), p. 922.
[71] Cf. MD 5, 1660f.

Without Mariology Christianity threatens imperceptibly to become inhuman. The Church becomes functionalistic, soulless, a hectic enterprise without any point of rest, estranged from its true nature by the planners, and because, in this manly-masculine world, all that we have is one ideology replacing another, everything becomes polemical, critical, bitter, humourless and ultimately boring, and people in their masses run away from such a Church.[72]

The Guardian of the Redeemer

The way for the Church to a truly Marian Christocentricity is a person. His name is Joseph:

> I am convinced that by reflecting upon the way that Mary's spouse shared in the divine mystery, the Church – on the road towards the future with all humanity – will be enabled to discover ever anew her own identity within this redemptive plan, which is founded on the mystery of the Incarnation.[73]

The 'Guardian of the Redeemer' has a unique place in the 'Christological constellation'. No one is closer to Mary, and so no one, after her, is closer to Jesus. With Mary, he is the first Guardian of the mystery of the Incarnation, the first to follow Mary on the pilgrimage of faith in the Word Incarnate.[74] His heavenly mission is the chivalrously male one of protecting the 'Marian profile' of the Church, of helping the faithful to learn this truth, the truth he lived: *The heart of the Mother holds the secret of the Son.*

---

[72] *Elucidations*, ET (London, 1975), p. 72.
[73] *Redemptoris Custos* 1; AAS 82 (1990), 6.
[74] Ibid., 6, 11.

6

The Saviour

Jesus Christ is the Redeemer of our race. John Paul II impresses the fact on our minds in the very titles of his documents: *Redemptor Hominis, Redemptoris Mater, Redemptoris Custos, Redemptoris Missio.* In 1983 he proclaimed a whole year in celebration of nineteen and a half centuries of the Redemption. When he invites us to 'open the doors for Christ', he is asking us to look up and see the slain Lamb in the midst of the throne. The central Christ is Saviour.

In his catechetical discourses the Holy Father followed the creeds by placing the Incarnation in the context of Redemption.[1] The Son of God becomes incarnate from the Virgin Mary 'for us men and for our salvation', that is to say, to liberate us from sin and from the death which came into the world through sin. Christological catechesis is therefore rightly prefaced by a tract on sin. To be truly Christocentric, we have to confront sin, men's actual sins here and now, but also the 'beginning' of the history of human sinfulness: the personal sin of Adam (*peccatum originale originans*), by which he lost the justice and holiness in which he had first been constituted, and the Original Sin which we contract through our descent from him (*peccatum originale originatum*).[2] John Paul II shares the conviction of his predecessor Pius XII that the greatest sin of the modern

[1] 'One could say that it is the interior logic of Revelation and of faith that impels us to concern ourselves in these catecheses above all with sin' (27/8/86; *Catechesi* 4, p. 13).

[2] On Original Sin, see *Catechesi* 4 , pp. 36–40.

age is the loss of the sense of sin.[3] We cannot fully appreciate the gift of salvation without weighing the gravity of sin, *quanti ponderis sit peccatum*.[4] To lose the sense of sin is to grow cold in thankful love of the Saviour.[5]

There is a mysterious interconnection between the treatises of dogmatic theology 'On the Word Incarnate' and 'On Sin'. On the one hand, it seems sensible to consider sin before the Incarnation, because the Word was made flesh to save sinners. On the other hand, it is only in the light of the Cross that we understand what sin truly is: sin is what crucifies God-made-man. The Cross, says the Pope, 'makes us understand the deepest roots of evil, which are fixed in sin and death'.[6] The slain Lamb bears the sins of the world, and so 'every sin, wherever and whenever committed, has a reference to the Cross – and therefore indirectly also to the sin of those who "have not believed in Him", and who condemned Jesus Christ to death on the Cross'.[7] It is our trespassses which, through Judas and Caiaphas and Pilate, through the soldiers and the crowd, nail Jesus to the Cross. However, we can only see this causal chain in light given by the Holy Spirit. As the Pope explains in *Dominum et Vivificantem*, it is the Paraclete who 'convinces the world concerning sin' (cf. John 16.7f.). In the hearts of men He demonstrates the connection of sin, every sin, with the Cross of Christ. He reveals it as the *mysterium iniquitatis*:

> Man does not know this dimension – he is absolutely ignorant of it – apart from the Cross of Christ. So he cannot be 'convinced' of it except by the Holy Spirit: the Spirit of truth, who is also the Counsellor.[8]

Without the Spirit's light, Adam's sons and daughters are blind to sin as sin. They begin to re-define the meaning of good and evil. Human wickedness ceases to be an offence to

---

[3] *Reconciliatio et Paenitentia* 18; AAS 77 (1985), 225. Cf. Pope Pius XII, *Discorsi e Radiomessaggi* 8 (Vatican City, 1946), p. 288.

[4] St Anselm cited on 28/9/83.

[5] Ibid.

[6] DM 8, 1204.

[7] DV 29, 840.

[8] DV 32, 844f. For those who follow the 'enlightened agenda', 'the Pope becomes *persona non grata* when he tries to convince the world of human sin' (*Crossing the Threshold of Hope* (New York, 1994), p. 57).

God's goodness, the force which drives nails into His beloved Son, and gets explained away as mental illness or social problem.

'Everything is manifested on the Cross', says St Bonaventure, God and man, the supreme beauty of holiness, the foul ugliness of sin.[9] It reveals, says Pope John Paul, both justice and mercy, the demand which turns out to be a staggeringly prodigal gift:

> The expiatory sacrifice of the Cross makes us understand the gravity of sin. In God's eyes sin is never a matter of no importance. The Father loves men and is profoundly offended by their transgressions or rebellions. Although disposed to pardon, yet for the good and honour of man himself, He asks for reparation. But it is precisely here that the divine generosity manifests itself in the most surprising way. The Father gives to mankind His own Son to offer this reparation. With this He shows all the abysmal gravity of sin, since He demands the highest possible reparation, that which comes from His own Son. At the same time He reveals the infinite greatness of His love, since He is the first, with the gift of His Son, to bear the burden of reparation.[10]

The Sinless Son Is Made Sin

The soteriology of Pope John Paul II is satisfyingly comprehensive. Themes in Scripture and Tradition neglected by theologians of recent generations – satisfaction, merit, substitution, victory over Satan – are recovered and revitalized.[11] There is not the space to consider each of these in detail. Instead I should like to consider three soteriological themes in which the similarities (and differences) between the teaching of the Holy Father and the theology of Balthasar are most apparent. The first of these is that hardest of hard texts: 'For our sake God made Him to be sin who knew no sin' (2 Cor. 5.21).

In expounding St Paul, the Holy Father – like Balthasar – develops the beautiful Patristic theology of the *admirable commercium*. The Son of God becomes the Son of Man in order to effect a 'wonderful exchange' between God and man. He takes our guilt in order to give us His innocence:

---

[9] *De Triplici Via* 3, 3; Quaracchi VIII, 14A.
[10] 20/4/83.
[11] Satisfaction, merit, sacrifice (20/4/83), victory over Satan (20/8/86, *Cathechesi* 3, pp. 149–153), substitution (26/10/88, *Catechesi* 9, pp. 27–33).

If He 'made to be sin' Him who was without any sin whatever, it was to reveal the love that is always greater than the whole of creation, the love that is He Himself, since God is love . . . This revelation of love is also described as mercy; and in man's history this revelation of love and mercy has taken a form and a name, that of Jesus Christ.[12]

The sin-bearing of the sinless Son manifests the infinite 'measure', the 'superabundance', of divine justice: this is how far the just God goes to deal with sin. But it also reveals the breathtaking proportions of divine mercy, 'the love that goes against what constitutes the very root of evil in the history of man: against sin and death'.[13] Mercy, 'love's second name', is the form in which Trinitarian love is revealed when, in the person of the incarnate Son, it meets evil in the world.[14]

When He makes His Son to be sin, the Father, says the Pope, not only manifests mercy, He invites it. Human co-operation with the Redemption is nothing other than the response of mercy to mercy. To 'open the doors' to Christ is to recognize Him, in an attitude of *pietà*, as the bearer of my burden:

> Christ, precisely as the Crucified One, is the Word that does not pass away (cf. Matt. 25.35), and He is the one who stands at the door and knocks at the heart of every man (cf. Rev. 3.20), without restricting his freedom, but instead seeking to draw from this very freedom love, which is not only an act of solidarity with the suffering Son of Man, but also a kind of 'mercy' shown by each one of us to the Son of the Eternal Father. In the whole of this messianic programme of Christ, in the whole revelation of mercy through the Cross, could man's dignity be more highly respected and ennobled, for, in obtaining mercy, He is in a sense the one who at the same time 'shows mercy'?[15]

The compassionate Mother at the foot of the Cross is, of course, the model and beginning of this Christ-ward mercy.[16]

Like Balthasar, the Pope has on many occasions meditated on the Cry of Dereliction. He believes it has a power to speak to

---

[12] RH 9, 273.
[13] DM 8, 1204.
[14] Ibid., 7, 1203.
[15] Ibid., 8, 1205.
[16] Ibid., 9, 1207f.

all men.[17] It is as Head, as our representative, that Christ voices the pain of every desolate and lost human being. Since He is a divine person, this action, like His every other human deed, has infinite saving power. By it He brings light into the blackest vault of human loneliness:

> One can say that these words of abandonment are born at the level of that inseparable union of the Son with the Father, and are born because the Father 'laid on Him the iniquity of us all' (Isa. 53.6). They also foreshadow the words of St Paul; 'For our sake He made Him to be sin who knew no sin' (2 Cor. 5.21). Together with this horrible weight, encompassing the 'entire' weight of the turning away from God which is contained in sin, Christ, through the divine depth of His filial union with the Father, perceives in a humanly inexpressible way this suffering which is separation, the rejection by the Father, the estrangement from God. But precisely through this suffering He accomplishes the Redemption, and can say as He breathes His last, 'It is accomplished' (John 19.30).[18]

The uncreated and sinless person of the Son in His humanity experiences a Godforsakenness, 'a mysterious affliction . . . In the interior recesses of the mind', which is more intense than anything a self-absorbed sinner could feel.[19] 'If sin is separation from God, Jesus had to experience in the crisis of His union with the Father, a suffering proportionate to that separation'.[20]

The Pope protects the Cry of Dereliction from exaggeration. The 'Why' of Jesus is not a protest, a voice of rebellion or despair:

> In the 'Why' of Jesus there is no feeling of resentment leading to rebellion or desperation; there is no semblance of a reproach to the Father, but the expression of the experience of weakness, of solitude, of abandonment to Himself, made by Jesus in our place; by Him who thus becomes the first of the 'smitten and afflicted', the first of the abandoned, the first of the *desamparados* (as the Spanish call them) . . .

The Holy Father appears at one point to draw on St Thomas's doctrine of Christ as *simul viator et comprehensor*.[21] He is at once

---

[17] Cf. RH 7, 269.
[18] SD 18; AAS 76 (1984), 224.
[19] 27/4/83.
[20] 30/11/88; *Catechesi* 9, p. 55.
[21] Cf. ST 3a 15, 10.

pilgrim and beholder, sufferer and seer, resting in the vision of the Father, yet afflicted by pain of body and soul surpassing anything endured or endurable by men:

> In fact, if Jesus feels abandoned by the Father, He knows however that that is not really so ... Dominant in His mind Jesus has the clear vision of God and the certainty of His union with the Father. But in the sphere bordering on the senses and therefore more subject to the impressions, emotions and influences of the internal experiences of pain, Jesus' human soul is reduced to a waste-land, and He no longer feels the 'presence' of the Father, but He undergoes the tragic experience of the most complete desolation.[22]

The Pope reads the Gospels in a Catholic way, that is to say, as a whole, without separating one from the others. Thus the Cry of Abandonment in Matthew and Mark is heard in dramatic harmony with the last words recorded by John and Luke: 'It is finished' (John 19.30) and 'Father, into thy hands I commit my spirit' (Luke 23.46). The incarnate Son bears even Godforsakeness 'in perfect harmony with the Father's will'.[23] Even when Father-forsaken, He is Father-centred. Even when desolate, He delivers Himself. This is the self-offering that makes our peace with God:

> There was a moment of desolation when Jesus felt without support and defence on the part of everyone, even of God; a dreadful moment, but it was soon overcome by entrusting Himself into the hands of the Father, whose loving and immediate presence Jesus realizes in the depths of His being, since He is in the Father as the Father is in Him (cf. John 10.38; 14.10f.), even on the Cross.[24]

There is no pain, no grief, like that of the Suffering Servant-Messiah, the crucified Son of God. No man has suffered, or could ever suffer, more intensely than God-made-man. In the words of Wojtyla the poet:

> But the depths of His words no one knows,
> No one knows how far
> The farthest reason goes,

[22] Ibid., p. 54.
[23] Ibid., pp. 58–62.
[24] Ibid., p. 60.

How limitless His suffering was –
Solitude on the tree of the Cross.[25]

The Descent into Hell

By including the Descent into Hell in his Christological catecheses, the Pope has helped restore it to its proper place in the theology of Redemption. With the whole tradition, he sees the words 'He descended into Hell' as teaching that Christ as man truly died. Having been separated from His body, Christ's soul went down into Sheol, the region of the dead. He has touched and transformed not only the act of dying but also the state of being dead. Unlike Balthasar, who tends to see the Descent primarily as an endurance, something suffered, the Pope shares the view of those theologians who hold that Christ's soul was immediately in the fullness of glory following its separation from the body and actively communicated its state of beatitude to the waiting souls of the just. The Descent is a true redeeming of the past, 'the super-historical mystery of the redemptive causality of Christ's humanity, the "instrument" of the omnipotent divinity'.[26]

The Resurrection

Jesus Christ is centre, but not dead centre. Having descended into Hell in His soul, He rose again in His body, and ascended into heaven in both.[27] The Cross is the still point of the turning world, but its pivotal power comes from the Resurrection:

> The whole world revolves around the Cross, but only in the Resurrection does the Cross reach its full significance of salvific event. The Cross and Resurrection constitute the one Paschal Mystery in which the history of the world is centred.[28]

If Christ is not risen, says St Paul, our faith is in vain (cf. 1 Cor. 15.14). No Easter, no Christianity. The Pope quotes Romano Guardini: 'With Jesus' Resurrection stands or falls

[25] Karol Wojtyla, *Collected Poems* (New York, 1982), p. 22.

[26] 11/1/89; *Catechesi* 9, p. 71f. See J. Galot SJ, *Jesus our Liberator*. A Theology of Redemption (Rome, 1982), pp. 330ff. On the Descent into Hell, see also CCC 631–637.

[27] Cf. the Fourth Lateran General Council (DS 801).

[28] 1/3/89; *Catechesi* 9, p. 99.

Christian faith'.[29] It is the supreme confirmation and crowning of all that Jesus did and taught 'from His birth to His Passion and Death, by His deeds, miracles, teaching, example of perfect holiness and especially by His transfiguration',[30] Above all, it confirms the truth of His divine identity as consubstantial Son of the Father: 'The Resurrection of the Crucified proved that He really was "I am" (cf. John 8.59), the Son of God.'[31]

Against all the demythologizing and etherealizing interpretations 'from Valentinus to Bultmann', the Pope reaffirms the historicity and bodiliness of the Resurrection.[32] The preaching of the Apostles is based on a 'real event', not a 'myth or conception'.[33] Of course, though truly historical, it is not just one event among many: it is the Event of events, in a certain sense 'transcending and standing above history'.[34] The Apostles did not invent the Resurrection. When Our Lord, after the Transfiguration, foretold His coming Resurrection, the disciples did not know what He was talking about (cf. Mark 9.9f.). They had been brought up to look forward to a general resurrection at the end of history, but they knew nothing of an anticipated resurrection. No Jew would be predisposed to fabricate such a belief, least of all eleven frightened Jews shattered by the 'extreme test' of their Master's execution.[35]

The Resurrection was bodily, the raising up of Jesus' body from the tomb. The empty tomb by itself was not a direct proof of the Resurrection: Mary Magdalene thought the emptiness meant that someone had taken the body. Nonetheless, for 'those of good will' it was 'a first step towards recognizing the fact of the Resurrection'.[36] The tomb was empty, they realized, because Jesus had Himself emptied it – by rising again in the flesh. When He appears to the disciples, the Lord reassures them

[29] R. Guardini, *The Lord*, ET (London, 1956), p. 406.
[30] 8/3/89; *Catechesi* 9, p. 105.
[31] Ibid., p. 102.
[32] 'From Valentinus to Bultmann this flesh and blood has been spiritualized and demythologized' (Balthasar, *The Glory of the Lord. A Theological Aesthetics*, vol. 1: Seeing the Form, ET (Edinburgh, 1982), p. 314).
[33] 1/2/89; *Catechesi* 9, p. 82.
[34] Ibid., p. 95.
[35] Ibid., p. 82f.
[36] Ibid., p. 86.

that He is no ghost, but gloriously alive in body, with flesh and bones (cf. Luke 25.36f.). The Risen One is the Crucified:

> He invites them to verify that the risen body in which He came to see them is the very same that was tortured and crucified. [The] body is authentic and real. In his material identity there is the proof of Christ's Resurrection.[37]

However, the risen body is wonderfully transformed. It is 'spiritual', which means that it 'shares in the soul's glory', is filled with the Holy Spirit's power, and is thus endowed with new properties.[38] When Jesus appears, He is the same and yet different, 'a "transformed" Christ'.[39] He has not returned to mortal earthly life, as Lazarus did, who had to do his dying all over again. No, Christ in His risen body has 'passed from death to "another" life beyond time and space'.[40]

The Pope makes the vitally important point, too often forgotten, that Christ's Resurrection confirms not only His full and complete divinity, but also His full and complete humanity. A Jesus 'risen' only in spirit would be a dead man, a departed soul, not a complete human being:

> The Resurrection confirms in a new way that Jesus is truly man. The Word was born in time 'by becoming flesh', and in the Resurrection He returned to life in His own human body. Only a true man could suffer and die on the Cross. Only a true man could rise from the dead. To rise again means to return to life in the body. Although transformed, endowed with new qualities and powers, and also glorified (as at Christ's Ascension and in the future resurrection of the dead), it is a truly human body . . . Finally, it is in this body, risen and now glorified, but always the body of a true man, that Christ ascends into heaven, to sit 'at the right hand of the Father'.[41]

The Resurrection of Jesus is the cause of our salvation. As the Pope says, 'the risen Christ is the principle and source of a new

[37] Ibid., p. 80.
[38] Ibid., p. 92.
[39] Ibid.
[40] Ibid., p. 96f.
[41] 27/1/88; *Catechesi* 7, p. 108.

life for everyone'.[42] This new life is the 'victory over the death caused by sin, and a sharing in the divine life of grace'.[43] First, in this life, there is what St Thomas, following the Fathers, would call the resurrection of the soul, which is divinization by grace. Then, at the end of time, there is the resurrection of the body, the completion of our divinization in glory. The pilgrim Church on earth, fed by the Body and Blood of the glorified Christ, is 'the true community of the resurrection'.[44] Her mission is in every way to 'oppose death' and thus co-operate with the Conqueror of Hades in His 'great uprising against death'.[45]

[42] 15/3/89; *Catechesi* 9, p. 107. See CCC 651–655.
[43] Ibid.
[44] Ibid., p. 109.
[45] Easter Sunday, 1986.

7

Cosmos in Christ

The history of heresy is a saga of false oppositions: unity of essence without distinction of persons (Sabellianism), distinction of persons without unity of essence (Arianism), freedom without grace (Pelagianism), grace without freedom (Calvinism). To demand a choice between a Creation-Christocentricity and a Redemption-Christocentricity would only add to the catalogue of wrong-headed alternatives. Pope John Paul II makes no such mistake. He teaches that the Son of God becomes man for the purpose of redemption, but he is also insistent that Christ, in His humanity as well as in His divinity, is 'the centre of the universe and of history'.[1]

Incarnation and Redemption
As we have seen, Pope John Paul's Christocentricity is soteriological. He nowhere even raises the hypothetical question of whether the Son of God would have become man in an unfallen world. Like St Thomas and St Bonaventure, he maintains an attitude of *pietas fidei*: he restrains speculation and modestly concentrates on what Scripture tells us of the mysterious will of God: 'Christ comes to save us. He is the Redeemer of man'.[2] The trouble with certain forms of Creation-Christocentricity is that, by weakening the Incarnation's link with Redemption, the hypostatic union can begin to look like the morally necessary climax of an inner-worldly process.

[1] RH 1, 257.
[2] 23/12/82.

55

Balthasar has warned against this tendency in the 'evolutionary' Christology of Karl Rahner.[3] Although Pope John Paul teaches that the incarnate Word and Redeemer is the centre and goal of the cosmos, he never forgets that the hypostatic union is pure unmerited gift, the grace of graces.[4] We must never become blasé in our thinking about Christ as crowning creation, as if this were 'only what might be expected' of God. The faith-enlightened mind must never lose its awe at what the Fathers boldly call the divine 'folly' of the Incarnation. 'It is by His foolish and infinite love', says St Maximus the Confessor, 'that He became truly and by nature the very thing He loved, without losing anything of His own nature in this ineffable self-emptying'.[5] This astonishment fills the Church's heart each year at the Easter Vigil. Creation is wonderful, but its re-creation in the incarnate Word, crucified and risen, is more amazing still:

How wonderful the condescension of thy kindness towards us!
What love and charity beyond reckoning!
To ransom a slave
thou gavest up thy Son!
O truly necessary sin of Adam blotted out by the death of Christ!
O happy fault that merited for us such and so great a Redeemer![6]

This sense of wonder runs through all the teaching of John Paul II. One word especially captures for him the prodigality of the Father's gift of the Son. The word is 'mercy'. The Pope's preoccupation with 'love's second name' protects his Christo-centric cosmology from any drift towards a mechanically necessary Incarnation.[7]

Cosmic Redemption

The Pope's Christocentricity is soteriological, but his soteriological Christocentricity is cosmic. When God the Son

---

[3] *Cordula, oder der Ernstfall*, 4th ed. (Einsiedeln, 1987), p. 90.
[4] Cf. St Thomas Aquinas, ST 3a 2, 10.
[5] *Ambigua* 5; PG 91. 1048C.
[6] The *Exsultet* of the Easter Vigil.
[7] The Redemption 'reveals the unheard-of greatness of man, *qui talem ac tantum meruit habere Redemptorem*' (DM 7, 1199).

becomes flesh from the flesh of the Virgin Mary, when He dies and rises again in that same flesh, He sets in motion the transfiguration of the whole material universe:

> The Incarnation of God the Son signifies the taking up into unity with God not only of human nature, but in this human nature, in a sense, of everything that is 'flesh'; the whole of humanity, the entire visible and material world. The Incarnation, then, also has a cosmic significance, a cosmic dimension. The 'first-born of all creation' (Col. 1.15), becoming incarnate in the individual humanity of Christ, unites Himself in some way with the entire reality of man, which is also 'flesh' (cf. Gen. 9.11, etc.) – and in this reality with all 'flesh', with the whole creation.[8]

Redemption is the outcome of the Creator's 'fidelity' towards human beings 'created in His image and chosen "from the beginning", in [His] Son, for grace and glory'.[9] Pope John Paul teaches explicitly that 'the incarnate Word, the Lord Jesus dead and risen' is the One 'in whom and in view of whom' man was created,[10] the final cause, 'the reason and cornerstone' of all creation.[11] It is precisely as incarnate Word and Redeemer that Jesus Christ is centre of the universe. In saying this, the Pope takes up many of the themes of the Fathers. As Irenaeus taught against the Gnostics, and as Athanasius and the Cappadocians argued against the Arians,[12] the Redeemer is the Creator, and His redemptive work is not the world's replacement, but its renewal and fulfilment. Redemption is re-creation.[13] St Thomas gladly follows the Fathers in this opinion,[14] and so does Pope John Paul. 'God

[8] DV 50, 870f.

[9] DV 7, 1200.

[10] 10/4/86.

[11] 5/3/86; *Catechesi* 3, p. 27.

[12] When the divine Word becomes man, He recapitulates His own handiwork (cf. St Irenaeus, *Adversus Haereses* 3, 18, 7; PG 7. 938B). Only the Creator can be Saviour (cf. St Athanasius, *Oratio 2 contra Arianos* 69; PG 25. 294A). The Word who made flesh is made flesh in Mary (cf. St Gregory of Nyssa, *Contra Eunomium* 4, 3; PG 45. 637B).

[13] 6/7/83.

[14] Through the Incarnation 'the whole divine work of [creating] the universe is in some way perfected, since man, who is created last, in a kind of circular movement returns to his principle, for he is united to the principle of things' (St Thomas Aquinas, *Compendium Theologiae* 201).

has re-created man in Christ, so that Christ has become the second and true Adam, who is at the origin of the new humanity'.[15] The eternal Word of God assumes human nature in order 'to bring about the fulfilment and redemption of the universal order'.[16]

In his poetry, Karol Wojtyla looks on material things as already transfigured in principle by the Word made flesh:

> I adore you, fragrant hay, because in you
> no pride ripens as in ears of corn;
> I adore you, fragrant hay, because you cuddled
> a barefoot baby, manger-born.[17]

Divinizing Redemption

Pope John Paul's soteriological Christocentricity is cosmic, because he has a broad definition of Redemption.[18] It is Redemption *for* as well as *from* something. Christ redeems us from sin and death and Satan, and redeems us for divinization, that is to say, for a share, in grace and glory, in the life of the Blessed Trinity. As St John Chrysostom says, 'what we received was not only a medicine to counteract the wound, but health and beauty and honour and glory and dignities far above our nature.'[19] The waters of Baptism are both a tomb and womb. We die to sin and are reborn to sonship. Through our incorporation into Christ we become by grace what He is by nature: we become sons-in-the-Son:

> The redemptive act has inserted the human person into Christ making him a sharer in the divine sonship of the Word: we are sons *in* the Only-Begotten Son of the Father. 'Since', as St Thomas writes, repeating the constant tradition of the Church, 'Christ

---

[15] 6/7/83.

[16] 17/3/91.

[17] Karol Wojtyla, *Collected Poems*, ET (New York, 1982), p. 11.

[18] Jesus frees us from the slavery of sin and for a new life (cf. 3/8/88, 10/8/88; *Catechesi* 8, 63–75). 'Salvation means above all liberation from evil and, in particular, liberation from sin, although it is obvious that the scope of this term is not reduced to this but embraces the riches of the divine life that Christ has brought to man' (27/8/86; *Catechesi* 4, p. 11).

[19] *In Epistolam ad Romanos Homiliae* 10; PG 60. 477.

received in His humanity the supreme fullness of grace, being the Only-Begotten of the Father, from Him grace flows to the others so that the Son of God made man makes men the sons of God'.[20]

This gift of divinizing adoption in the eternal Son, which comes to the fallen sons of Adam as a healing as well as elevating grace, is the supernatural destiny which God has planned for man from before the foundation of the world (cf. Eph. 1.3–10):

> The creative Wisdom that is the measure of all reality, in the Truth of which every creature is true, has a name: the Incarnate Word, the Lord Jesus dead and risen. In Him and in view of Him man is created, because the Father – in His utterly free plan – has wanted man to participate, in the Only-Begotten Son, in the Trinitarian life itself.[21]

The divinizing grace of the incarnate Son transfigures the whole man. The final flowering of humanity, for which even the souls of the blessed yearn, is the resurrection of the body.[22] This will be a 'spiritualization' of the body in the sense that the soul will 'dominate' and 'fully permeate' the body; the 'war' between flesh and spirit will be ended (cf. Rom. 7.21);[23] but it will not be in any sense a 'disincarnation of the body' or a 'dehumanization of man'.[24] It will be the fulfilment of man, his body's supreme beautification. And not only of man: the general resurrection will be the transfiguration of the whole material order (cf. Rom. 8.22f.).[25] We can understand now the words of St Maximus:

> The mystery of the Incarnation contains in itself all the meaning of the enigmas and symbols of Scripture, all the significance of creatures, visible and intelligible. The one who knows the mystery of the Cross and Burial apprehends the inward essences

[20] 12/8/83.
[21] 10/4/86.
[22] St Thomas says that the desire of the blessed soul for an object is wholly satisfied in God. Nevertheless, it does not possess its object in every way it could wish, and so when it regains the body in the resurrection, its happiness will gain in extent, though not in intensity (cf. ST 1a2ae 4, 5, ad 4 & 5). Dante takes up the idea in the *Paradiso* (14, 43ff.).
[23] Cf. 9/12/81.
[24] 9/12/81.
[25] Cf. 21/7/82.

of created things. The one initiated into the hidden significance of the Resurrection knows the end for which God from the beginning created all things.[26]

A Trinitarian Cosmology

The centring of the cosmos on Christ can only be properly understood in a Trinitarian context. In the catecheses of Spring 1986, Pope John Paul developed a richly Trinitarian account of creation. His starting-point is the axiom common to St Thomas and St Bonaventure and re-asserted in our own time by Balthasar: *Only a Trinitarian God could be Creator*. As St Bonaventure says, 'God could not have produced creatures by will had He not produced the Son by nature'.[27] There can only be essential difference outside the Godhead because there is personal difference inside the Godhead. The Son who is uncreated Image of the Father is also the exemplar of creatures. As Word, says St Thomas, He is purely expressive of the Father and both expressive and causative of creatures.[28] Pope John Paul argues on similar lines:

> The world was created by the Word in union with the Father (and the Holy Spirit). The Son–Word, who is the Image of the Father, 'reflecting the glory of God and bearing the very stamp of His nature' (cf. Heb. 1.3), is also 'He who is the first-born of all creation' (Col. 1.15), in the sense that all things have been created in the Word–Son to become, in time, the world of creatures called from nothingness into existence 'outside God'.[29]

We have to read the book of creation in a Trinitarian way. Since the world was created by the Father through His Word–Image, it has a 'logical' and 'iconic' structure; its rationality and order are a reflection of the uncreated Wisdom. Creatures are 'words of the Word' and indeed 'gifts of the Gift', because they were created by the Father through the Logos of Wisdom and in the Spirit of Love.[30]

[26] *Capitum Theologicorum et Oeconomicorum Duae Centuriae* 1, 66; PG 90. 1108AB.
[27] St Bonaventure, *Commentarium super librum I Sententiarum* dist. 7, dub. 2; Quaracchi I, 144B. Cf. Balthasar, TD 4, 53–57.
[28] Cf. St Thomas, ST 1a 34, 3.
[29] 5/3/86; *Catechesi* 3, p. 28.
[30] Ibid., p. 29.

This demonstrates that all things were created in and for Christ as God, that is to say, in and for the Son with the Father and the Holy Spirit. Does it sufficiently explain the sense in which creation is directed towards Him in His crucified and risen humanity? I want to answer that question by glossing John Paul II with the help of the insights of Balthasar and Bouyer.

If we are to understand how Christ as man, as Redeemer, can be the One in whom the cosmos was created, we must remember that the Blessed Trinity wills and effects the temporal world's creation, redemption, and consummation *eternally*. There are no 'moments' in the everlasting Now of God, though no moment of time is 'outside His eternal embrace'.[31] In a single, simple, eternal act, the Triune God creates free creatures, angels and men, with the super-natural destiny of adoptive sonship, permits the sin of Lucifer and Adam, unites human nature to the person of the Son so that He can make satisfaction for human sin and destroy the works of the Devil, raises His human body from the tomb, and in Him, at the end of time, brings the whole universe to its fulfilment.[32] As C. S. Lewis says, 'God saw the Crucifixion in the act of creating the first nebula'.[33] If the divine act of uniting human nature to the Son is eternal (though the nature united is temporal), then the Father does indeed look eternally on the human face of His Son, and so He can truly be said to create the world in view of Him as man, even as Babe of Bethlehem, even as crucified and risen from the tomb. All things were created eternally by the Father, in the Spirit, through the Son who in 'the fullness of time' became man to recapitulate all things in Himself. Hans Urs von Balthasar has said it all very well:

[31] 4/9/85 on the eternity of God; *Catechesi* 2, p. 47.

[32] 'As far as God is concerned, He creates us eternally. He sends us the Son and the Spirit eternally. It is eternally that He decides our adoption in the Son, the Son's redemptive Incarnation, and the fulfilment of all things in the gift of the Spirit bestowed on every creature in the Only-Begotten. It is eternally that He knows and loves us, and thus knowing and loving us, He eternally makes us to be all that we are called to be in time' (Louis Bouyer, *Cosmos. Le monde et la gloire de Dieu* (Paris, 1982), p. 305).

[33] *The Problem of Pain*, new ed. (London, 1957), p. 72.

The New Testament hymns (John 1, Eph. 1, Col. 1) are agreed that the cosmos as a whole . . . was created by the Logos (together with God), and not by a *Logos asarkos*, but by the Son of God who from eternity was predestined to be made flesh. 'Without Him was not anything made that was made' (John 1.3). 'In Him all things hold together' (Col. 1.17). This One who at the beginning is Creator of all will also be, in the fullness of time, the Redeemer of all. It is God's plan to guide and lead the course of history to the Incarnation in order 'to sum up all things under Christ as Head, things in heaven and things on earth' (Eph. 1.10).[34]

[34] Balthasar, *Epilog* (Einsiedeln & Trier, 1987), p. 7.

8

The Church of Christ

A truly Catholic Christocentricity does not separate Christ from His Church. In 1975, in *Evangelii Nuntiandi,* Pope Paul VI stated this maxim with the utmost vigour. It is absurd, he said, to claim to love and listen to Christ but without the Church, to belong to Christ but outside the Church. There cannot, therefore, be authentic evangelization without the Church.[1] Pope John Paul has spoken with equal firmness:

> With Scripture and Tradition . . . we must insist on the unbreakable bond that exists between Christ and His Church, between the Bridegroom and His Bride, between the Head and His members, between the Mother and her spiritual children.[2]

The splendour of Christ shines upon the face of His Church. The light of His truth, scattering the darkness of our minds, is radiated by His Bride. Christ is the answer to all man's questions, and the Church offers that answer to the world.[3] It is in and through the Church that man can encounter Christ.[4]

The ecclesial character of true Christocentricity has important ecumenical implications. If Jesus and His Church are inseparable, if He is truly the founder of the Church and her ministerial and sacramental structure,[5] then ecclesiological disagreement

---

[1] Cf. *Evangelii Nuntiandi* 16; AAS 68 (1975), 16.
[2] 23/11/87.
[3] Cf. VS 2.
[4] 'In order to make this "encounter" with Christ possible, God willed His Church' (VS 6).
[5] Cf. 15/6/86, 22/6/88, 13/7/88; *Catechesi* 8, pp. 39–56.

will always be in a certain sense Christological. During his visit to Germany in 1980, speaking of the persisting difficulties between Catholics and Lutherans, the Holy Father said that if they really were only 'ecclesiastical prescriptions of human institution', as the Augsburg Confession claims, they could and should be eliminated immediately. But they are not: the clash concerns Christ:

> According to the conviction of Catholics, the dissent turns on 'that which is of Christ', on 'that which is His', namely His Church and her mission, her message, her Sacraments and her ministries ordained to the service of the Word and of the Sacrament.[6]

Forty years ago, in a regrettably neglected essay, Father Yves Congar OP suggested that Luther's theology of grace, which excluded the possibility of the Church's and Mary's co-operation with Christ, derived from an essentially Mono-thelite Christology, according to which, in the person of the Word incarnate Himself, the divine will overwhelms and swallows up the human, robbing it of its freedom.[7] Similarly, Balthasar, in his study of Karl Barth, suggests that the Protestant refusal of 'the Catholic "and"' derives from a Christological deficiency:

> The attempt of Karl Barth and the theologians closest to him to connect the distinctive Catholic doctrines at all costs with the (philosophical) *analogia entis* is mistaken, unless by *analogia entis* one means the compatibility, shown once and for all in Christ, of divine nature and human nature. In Christ human nature is not ground under by the divine; it is given a chance to serve. In the Church this service is always prompted, supported, made possible, and directed by grace . . . Whether we are talking about Church structures (e.g. the infallible teaching office and the grace 'contained' in the sacraments), or ecclesial man's 'co-operation' with grace (e.g. in the doctrine of 'merit' and 'sanctity', including its consequences in Mariology), we are really talking about God's free use through Christ of man and the human order . . . The very

---

[6] 17/11/80.
[7] Cf. Y. Congar OP, 'Regards et réflexions sur la christologie de Luther', in A. Grillmeier and H. Bacht (edd.), *Das Konzil von Chalkedon*, vol. 3 (Würzburg, 1954), p. 468f.

things in the Catholic Church which the Protestant reproachfully regards as human interference are, for the Church herself, the supreme condescension of God's grace.[8]

A Nuptial Christocentricity
The ecclesial Christocentricity of Pope John Paul II is more precisely *nuptial*. He invites us to look on the central Christ with the devoted eyes of a bride, of *the* Bride, the Church. In the words of the mysterious figure of Adam in Wojtyla's play *The Jeweller's Shop*, 'the Bridegroom is coming down this street and walks every street! How am I to prove to you that you are the bride?' Taking up a great Patristic theme, the Pope encourages each individual believer to assume the bridal attitude of the Church, to be an *anima ecclesiastica*. 'All human beings – both women and men – are called, through the Church, to be the "Bride" of Christ, the Redeemer of the world.'[9] Christ's redemptive love has a spiritually spousal character.[10] The Redeemer is husband of the redeemed, which is why His maleness is an essential aspect of revelation:

> The Bridegroom – the Son consubstantial with the Father as God – became the Son of Mary; He became the 'Son of Man', true man, a male. The symbol of the Bridegroom is masculine. This masculine symbol represents the human aspect of the divine love which God has for Israel, for the Church, and for all people.[11]

First in his ethical and dramatic work and then in his official teaching, Pope John Paul II has done what M. J. Scheeben in the nineteenth century and Balthasar in the twentieth have tried to do in their theological syntheses: he has restored the nuptial mystery to its proper centrality in the understanding of faith.[12]

---

[8] *Karl Barth*. Darstellung und Deutung seiner Theologie (Einsiedeln, 1976), p. 394f.

[9] MD 25, 1713f. For the quotation from *The Jeweller's Shop*, see Karol Wojtyla, *The Collected Plays and Writings on Theater*, ET (Berkeley, 1987), p. 305.

[10] 8/9/82.

[11] MD 25, 1714.

[12] On the nuptial mystery, see M. J. Scheeben, *Die Mysterien des Christentums*, new ed. (Freiburg, 1941), pp. 446ff.; and Balthasar, *Sponsa Verbi* (Einsiedeln, 1961), especially 'Wer ist die Kirche?' (pp. 148–292) and 'Casta Meretrix' (pp. 203–305).

Before delivering his extensive commentary on *Humanae Vitae* in 1984, the Pope gave five General Audience addresses on the 'great analogy', that is to say, on the union of husband and wife as the image of the spiritual covenant between God and man, between Christ and His Church.[13] This included a commentary, in the spirit of the Fathers and the great medieval theologians, on the Song of Songs. Not since St Gregory the Great has this been attempted by a Pope.

If John Paul's Christocentricity is nuptial, his theology of marriage is Christocentric. The Incarnation and the Redemption are 'the definitive source of the sacramentality of marriage'.[14] Like Balthasar, so it seems to me, the Pope holds that what gives the Sacrament of Matrimony its distinctive form,[15] what shapes it to be what it is, is the spiritual union of Christ and His Church:

> By virtue of the sacramentality of their marriage, spouses are bound to one another in the most profoundly indissoluble manner. Their belonging to each other is the real representation, by means of the sacramental sign, of the very relationship of Christ with the Church. Spouses are therefore the permanent reminder to the Church of what happened on the Cross; they are for one another and for the children witnesses to the salvation in which the sacrament makes them sharers.[16]

It is, of course, not only the Sacrament of Marriage which enables human beings to share in the nuptial mystery. Baptism inserts each one of us into 'the spousal covenant of Christ and the Church',[17] and the Eucharist and the supreme 'Sacrament of our Redemption' is also 'the Sacrament of the Bridegroom and Bride', making present and realizing anew in a sacramental manner 'the redemptive act of Christ the Bridegroom towards the Church the Bride'.[18] That is why the priest, acting in the

---

[13] Cf. 23/5/84, 30/5/84, 6/6/84.

[14] 2/4/80.

[15] 'Form' is being used here in its general metaphysical, rather than strictly sacramental, sense.

[16] FC 13; AAS 74 (1982), 95. For Balthasar on the Sacrament of Marriage, see *A Theology of History*, ET (London, 1964), p. 93, and *The Glory of the Lord* 1, p. 576f.

[17] FC 13, 95.

[18] MD 26, 1716.

person of Christ, has to be male.[19] Virginity or celibacy for the sake of the Kingdom is also a participation in the spousal covenant.[20] In *Mulieris Dignitatem* the Pope says that, whatever her state of life, every Christian woman is in some sense married, 'either through the Sacrament of Marriage or spiritually through marriage to Christ'. In both cases, marriage means 'the "sincere gift of the person" of the Bride to the Groom'.[21]

The nuptial–ecclesial Christocentricity of Pope John Paul II sheds light on the phenomenon of dissent from the Church's living Magisterium. It seems to me that this Promethean mentality is the tragic consequence of losing the feminine sense of the Church as Bride and Mother. Dissident theologians tend to see the Church as an oppressive impersonal organization, an It, something to protest against. By contrast, the great Catholic Doctors see the Church embodied in Mary, and so they see It as She, a woman, a mother, someone to be protected by. They gratefully and gladly say Yes to the Church's teaching, because they know that, amidst the shifting sands of the world's fads and fancies, it offers solid, Christ-provided rock, the only sure foundation for human lives. To 'think with the Church' is to think in devoted union with one who is 'our holy Mother' and 'Christ our Lord's undoubted Spouse'.[22]

---

[19] Ibid. See chapter 13 below.
[20] Cf. FC 16, 98f.; MD 20, 1702ff.
[21] MD 21, 1705.
[22] Cf. St Ignatius Loyola, *Spiritual Exercises*, ET, T. Corbishley SJ (London, 1963), p. 120 (n. 353).

9

The Eucharistic Christ

For Pope John Paul II, Christocentricity is not a mere concept, a theme in theology. It is the living Jesus Himself – body, blood, soul and divinity – at the centre of His Church, on her altars, in the Eucharist:

> Jesus is not an idea, a sentiment, a memory! Jesus is a person, always alive and present with us! Love Jesus present in the Eucharist. He is present in a sacrificial way in Holy Mass, which renews the Sacrifice of the Cross. To go to Mass means going to Calvary to meet Him, our Redeemer. He comes to us in Holy Communion and remains present in the tabernacles of our churches, for He is our friend.[1]

The Holy Father's Eucharistic preaching has an extraordinary power. Like the Curé of Ars, to whom he devoted one of his Holy Thursday letters, he centres the faithful on Christ by pointing them to the Altar of Sacrifice, to the Tabernacle of Presence. We have no abstract Redeemer, no absent Lord: 'He is here!'[2] In Orvieto in 1990, on the Solemnity of Corpus Christi, he centred his congregation on the Eucharistic Christ with these dramatic words:

> We are facing Christ really present under the veil of ordinary and material appearances, Christ–Bread, Christ–Wine.[3]

The Eucharistic teaching of the Pope has that Petrine completeness and balance, that Catholicity of vision, already

[1] 8/11/78.
[2] Holy Thursday 1986.
[3] 17/6/90.

69

noted in his more general Christocentricity. In *Redemptor Hominis* he reminded the faithful that the Eucharist is always and 'at one and the same time a Sacrifice-Sacrament, a Communion-Sacrament, and a Presence-Sacrament'.[4] He has re-stated the Council of Trent's teaching on the Eucharistic Sacrifice with particular verve. In the Mass, he says, 'the bloody sacrifice of Christ is continually renewed and is once more made present'.[5] Acting in the person of Christ, priests 're-enact and apply the one Sacrifice of the New Testament'.[6] The whole Church is caught up into the Sacrifice of her Lord: the Mass is simultaneously both 'the Sacrifice of Christ and the Sacrifice of the Church, because in the Eucharist Christ unites the Church with His own redemptive work, making it participate in His offering'.[7] Christ's Sacrifice on the Cross is not locked away in the dead archives of history. In the Mass, in the words of the prophet, it is 'revived in the midst of the years' (Hab. 3.2), daily renewed, perpetuated, earthed in the here-and-now:

> And how can we not feel intimately moved at the thought that that 'offering of His own body' for us is not a long-ago act, committed to the cold pages of historical chronicles, but it is an event that is still alive even now, although in an unbloody way, in the Sacrament of the Body and Blood, placed on the table of the altar? Christ returns to offer His Body and His Blood for us now, so that the purifying wave of divine mercy may spread once more over the misery of our condition as sinners, and that the seed of immortal life may be placed in the frailty of our mortal flesh.[8]

This ever-newness of Christ's Sacrifice in the Mass is made possible by, is a participation in, the eternal Now of the Triune God:

> Yes, the Sacrifice of the Son is unique and irreplaceable. It was accomplished only once in the history of humanity. Yet this unique and irreplaceable Sacrifice 'remains'. The event of Golgotha belongs to the past. The reality of the Trinity constitutes

[4] RH 20, 312.
[5] 8/6/87. 'The Eucharist is a sacrifice ... because it makes present the Sacrifice of the Cross, because it is its memorial, and because it applies its fruit' (CCC 1366).
[6] 5/5/84.
[7] 1/6/83.
[8] 8/10/88.

an eternal divine 'today'. This is why the whole of humanity can participate in this 'today' of the Son's sacrifice. The Eucharist is the sacrament of this unfathomable 'today'. The Eucharist is the sacrament – the greatest the Church has – through which the divine 'today' of the Redemption of the world meets our human 'today' in an ever new way.[9]

Pope John Paul can truly say, with St Irenaeus: 'Our opinion is in harmony with the Eucharist; the Eucharist confirms our thinking'.[10] This most Blessed Sacrament is the complete recapitulation of everything that is meant by Christocentricity, that attitude which is at once Trinitarian, Marian, soteriological, cosmic, ecclesial. The Eucharist is the whole of Christianity, the Church's entire commonwealth, because it is the central Jesus.

[9] 8/10/88.
[10] *Adversus Haereses* 4, 18, 4–5; PG 7. 1028A.

PART III

Christ the Answer

10

Man Revealed in Christ

According to the Second Vatican Council, in its *Pastoral Constitution on the Church in the Modern World*, Our Lord Jesus Christ, true God made true man, *reveals* both God and man. The section 'On Christ the New Man' makes Christology the key to theological anthropology. No conciliar text has been more frequently quoted by the present Pope:

> Only in the mystery of the Word made flesh does the mystery of man become clear. For Adam, the first man, was a type of Him who was to come (cf. Rom. 5.14), Christ the Lord. Christ the New Adam, in the very revelation of the mystery of the Father and of His love, fully reveals man to himself and so brings to light his most high calling . . . He who is the 'image of the invisible God' (cf. Col. 1.15) is Himself the perfect man who has restored in the children of Adam that likeness to God which had been disfigured ever since the first sin. Human nature, by the very fact that it was assumed, not absorbed, in Him has been raised in us also to a dignity beyond compare. For, by His Incarnation, the Son of God has in a certain way united Himself with every man. He worked with human hands, He thought with a human mind, He acted with a human will, and with a human heart He loved. Born of the Virgin Mary, He has truly been made one of us, like to us in all things except sin.[1]

The Council's Christocentric doctrine of man was re-asserted by the Pope in many of his early addresses.[2] It is the major

[1] GS 22; *Decreta*, p. 709. Cf. CCC 359.
[2] For example, in the address at Puebla in January 1979; at the meeting with the members of the International Theological Commission in October 1979; and at the Angelicum in November 1979.

75

premise of his argument in several encyclicals[3] and apostolic letters, and constantly, in his daily teaching, it continues to re-appear.[4] The most detailed exposition of Christ's revealing of man was in the Pope's first encyclical, *Redemptor Hominis* Without the incarnate Word, he said, human beings cannot decipher the enigma of their humanity:

> The man who wishes to understand himself thoroughly – and not just in accordance with immediate, partial, often superficial, and even illusory standards and measures of his being – he must with his unrest, uncertainty, and even his weakness and sinfulness, with his life and death, draw near to Christ. He must, so to speak, enter into Him with all his own self, he must 'appropriate' and assimilate the whole of the reality of the Incarnation and Redemption in order to find himself. If this profound process takes place within him, he then bears fruit not only of adoration of God but also of deep wonder at himself. How precious must man be in the eyes of the Creator, if he 'gained so great a Redeemer', and if God gave His only Son in order that man should not perish but have eternal life (cf. John 3.16).[5]

The ideas expressed here are already discernible in Karol Wojtyla's pre-papal career: for example in his study of Vatican II, *Sources of Renewal*, and in the 1976 Vatican retreat conferences, *Sign of Contradiction*, in which he shows that Christ's revealing of man is not a theory, not an ideology, but a fact, 'the fact that by His Incarnation the Son of God united Himself with every man, became man Himself, one of us, "like us in all things except sin" (Heb. 4.15)'.[6] God reveals man to man by becoming man. God-made-man is the perfect man, the norm and paradigm of what it is to be human, the Man, as Wojtyla the poet says, 'in whom each man can find his deep design, and the roots of his deeds'.[7]

The Christ-centredness of the Church's teaching about man is not just a topic for academic scrutiny. It is the Good News to

---

[3] Cf. VS 2.

[4] For example, addressing the bishops of the ninth pastoral region in the USA (8/7/88).

[5] RH 10, 274.

[6] Karol Wojtyla, *Sign of Contradiction*, ET (Slough, 1979), p. 102; *Sources of Renewal*, ET (London, 1980), p. 75.

[7] *Collected Poems*, ET (New York, 1982), p. 122.

be conveyed to the ends of the earth, to every human being: God-made-man alone makes sense of human life. To evangelize means helping a person 'to see himself in Christ, to find again in Him the true meaning of his own life, simply to find himself again in Christ'.[8] Perhaps the most straightforward and touching articulation of the idea was in the Pope's address to the young people of Great Britain in 1982. Christ's revelation of the truth about man, he explained, has to be received in prayer:

In prayer, united with Jesus – your brother, your friend, your Saviour, your God – you begin to breathe a new atmosphere. You form new goals and new ideals. Yes, in Christ, you begin to understand yourselves more fully. This is what the Second Vatican Council wanted to emphasize when it stated: 'The truth is that only in the mystery of the Incarnate Word does the mystery of man take on light'. In other words, Christ not only reveals God to man, but He reveals man to himself. In Christ we grasp the secret of our humanity.[9]

A Theocentric–Christocentric Anthropology
The general attributes already noted in Pope John Paul's Christocentricity are found once again in this anthropology. It is theocentric, Trinitarian, as well as Christocentric. In *Centesimus Annus*, he quotes Paul VI: 'In order to know man, authentic man, man in his fullness, one must know God'.[10] Man is great because he is made in the image of the ever greater God. He is raised to a grandeur beyond compare because His nature has been assumed, without absorption, by the Son of God. It takes God as man to show man what he truly is and to make him be what he is meant to be. The light shed by Christ on man comes from above, but it shines from within His own true humanity. His human face, the face wiped by Veronica, is 'the land of deepest meaning'.[11]

The Pope's theocentric–Christocentric anthropology makes use of the Patristic and medieval theology of image and like-

[8] 14/2/79.
[9] 2/6/82.
[10] CA 58.
[11] Cf. the poem 'Veronica' in Karol Wojtyla, *Collected Poems*, ET (New York, 1982), p. 162.

ness. He points out that rational creatures are only 'in' or 'to' the image of God,[12] whereas the uncreated Word *is* the Image of the Father, His perfect Expression. This means that man has a special relationship with the Second Person of the Blessed Trinity:

> Man created in the image of God acquires, in God's plan, a special relationship with the Word, the Father's Eternal Image, who in the fullness of time will become flesh.[13]

Man is 'logical', a rational creature, because he is ordered in a certain way towards the uncreated Logos. To be 'in the image of God', therefore, is to be in a state of 'tension towards full openness to the truth', to the One who is Truth in His very person.[14] And since the Image–Truth–Word is also Son, to be made in God's image is to be shaped for the destiny of sonship: 'Those whom [God the Creator] foreknew He also predestined to be conformed to the image of His Son, in order that He might be the first-born of many brethren' (Rom. 8.29). In one of his catecheses the Pope said:

> The truth about man created in the image of God does not merely determine man's place in the whole order of creation, but it already speaks even of his link with the order of salvation in Christ, who is the eternal and consubstantial 'Image of God' (cf. 2 Cor. 4.4), the Image of the Father. Man's creation in the image of God, from the very beginning of the Book of Genesis, bears witness to his call. This call is fully revealed with the coming of Christ.[15]

We can now see why Christ reveals man and his high calling *in and through* the revelation of the Father and His love.[16] The consubstantial Son, who is both the Father's Image and man's exemplar, becomes man in the Blessed Virgin's womb, teaches and heals, suffers and dies and rises from the tomb, in order to restore man to loving communion with the Father in the Holy Spirit. Man's 'high calling' is sonship-in-the-Son.

[12] 'Man is only a very imperfect image of God' (citing St Thomas, 25/1/84).
[13] 9/4/86; *Catechesi* 3, p. 48.
[14] 25/1/84.
[15] 9/4/86; *Catechesi* 3, p. 48.
[16] DM 1, 1178f.

A Dignity Beyond Compare

According to *Gaudium et Spes*, 'human nature, by the very fact that it was assumed, not absorbed, in Him has been raised in us also to a dignity beyond compare'. As is made clear in a footnote, this is an application of the teaching of Chalcedon and the two ecumenical councils that followed it.[17] Human nature is not destroyed, swallowed up or impaired by its hypostatic union with the divine person of the Word but perfected, sanctified, given a new and unequalled dignity. Moreover, since Christ is our Head and consubstantial with us in humanity, we can say that human nature 'in us also' is elevated. It is truly our common humanity which in Him is exalted. The astounding nobility bestowed on man by the eternal Son's assumption of his nature is the constant theme of the preaching of the Fathers. As St Leo the Great tells his Christmas congregation, 'Wake up, O man, and recognize the dignity of your nature. Remember that you were made in the image of God, the image which, deformed in Adam, is reformed in Christ'.[18] Pope John Paul takes up his predecessor's clarion call:

In Christ and through Christ God has revealed Himself fully to mankind and has definitively drawn close to it; at the same time, in Christ and through Christ man has acquired full awareness of his dignity, of the heights to which he is raised, of the surpassing worth of his own humanity, and of the meaning of his existence.[19]

The Incarnation and the Human Body

Matter is good, created by God, and a part of our human nature. Through the Incarnation and bodily Resurrection of God the Son, it has been raised to a nobility beyond the earth-bound materialist's wildest imaginings. *Regnat Deus Dei caro*. It is this truth which underlies the Pope's remarkable 'theology of the body'. When the Word was made flesh, the body, all matter, entered theology 'through the main door'.[20]

In his interview with Angelo Scola, Balthasar expressed the opinion that the Pope's 'thoughts concerning the body' are of

[17] GS 22; *Decreta*, p. 710n.
[18] Pope St Leo the Great, *In Nativitate Domini* 7, 5; SC 22B, 160.
[19] RH 11, 277.
[20] 2/4/80.

the greatest contemporary relevance because of the continuing influence of various kinds of spiritualism, all of which hold that true religion must be a flight from the body.[21] The religion of the Incarnation, by contrast, believes that the flesh is the 'hinge of salvation'. In the light of the Word made flesh, the body of every man can be seen more clearly as the 'manifestation' of spirit, the expression of the acting person, the means of dialogue and communion.[22] In its masculinity and femininity it speaks a language, and that language is marriage:

> As ministers of a sacrament which is constituted by consent and perfected by conjugal union, man and woman are called to express that mysterious 'language' of their bodies in all the truth which is proper to it. By means of gestures and reactions, by means of the whole dynamism, reciprocally conditioned, of tension and enjoyment – whose direct source is the body in its masculinity and its femininity, the body in its action and reaction – by means of all this, man, the person, 'speaks'.[23]

Christ United to Every Man

In *Redemptor Hominis* Pope John Paul develops the teaching of *Gaudium et Spes* that 'by His Incarnation the Son of God has in a certain way united Himself with each man'. This is a re-statement of the classical theology of the headship of Christ from St Paul and St Irenaeus to St Thomas, what Balthasar calls the mystery of 'inclusion in Christ'.[24] God the Son becomes man to put an end to the sinful fragmentation of our race. He is sent by the Father to recapitulate mankind, to draw every man into unity with Himself and so with His Father and one another:

> We are not dealing with the 'abstract' man, but the real, 'concrete', 'historical' man. We are dealing with 'each' man, for each one is included in the mystery of the Redemption and with each one Christ has united Himself for ever through this mystery. Every

---

[21] Cf. *Test Everything: Hold Fast to What is Good*. An Interview with Hans Urs von Balthasar by Angelo Scola, ET (San Francisco, 1989), p. 80.

[22] Cf. 22/10/80. Cf. *The Acting Person*, ET (Dordrecht, Boston & London, 1979), p. 204f.

[23] 22/8/84.

[24] TD 2/2, pp. 211–238.

In reducing modern day religions who deal w/ flight from the body we have the Incarnation whose flesh is the hinge.

man comes into the world through being conceived in his mother's womb and being born of his mother, and precisely on account of the mystery of the Redemption is entrusted to the solicitude of the Church.[25]

If modern theology is to appropriate this delicate and easily misunderstood doctrine, it would be advised to draw on the wisdom of the great post-Chalcedonian Greek Fathers, St Maximus the Confessor, St John Damascene, and St Theodore the Studite, who taught the universality of Jesus Christ without any compromise of His particularity. Their great insight is that the hypostatic union guarantees both the individuality and the inclusiveness of Christ as man. It is in the Trinitarian hypostasis of the Son that His human nature is 'enhypostatized', given concrete existence; but precisely because He is a divine person, not just another human person come to swell the ranks of sinful mankind, He enjoys in His human nature an incomparable capacity for communion. Precisely because He is One of the Trinity, He can be one of us without exclusion, without opposition to the rest of us, and thus He can bear, and bear away, the sins of all on the Cross.[26]

Christ and Personhood

The distinction between 'person' and 'nature', though comprehensible to every man by the light of reason, is the achievement of the Christian theological tradition. It was first worked out, in the fourth and fifth centuries, in connection with the Three Divine Persons and the Incarnation of the Second, and only later applied to created subjects. It is not transported from Greek philosophy. As Pope John Paul said in one of his Christological catecheses, Chalcedon 'adopted those concepts and terms from the current language, without reference to a particular philosophical system'.[27] *Hypostasis* had a bewildering variety of everyday and philosophical meanings, as did *physis* and *ousia*. *Prosôpon* meant 'theatrical mask', hence 'character', hence 'person' in the externally visible sense. None of the pagan

[25] RH 13, 283.
[26] See my article 'Christ, Our Lady, and the Church in the Teaching of the Second Council of Nicaea', *Chrysostom* 8 (1988), 13f.
[27] 16/3/88; *Catechesi* 7, p. 146.

systems of philosophy had grasped the metaphysical irreducibility of hypostasis to essence, of person to nature.[28] 'Even linguistically', suggested Christiane Morati, 'it needed a God, an incarnate God, to bring "person" to the fore'.[29] Only when the Three-Personed God revealed Himself in Christ did the beauty of personhood dawn on the wounded intellect of man. Pope John Paul has developed this argument:

> Here it should be noted that, with the doctrine concerning the divine Person of the Word–Son who assumed human nature and thereby entered the world of human persons, the Council emphasized the dignity of the man-person and the relations existing between various persons . . . How can one not see in this the point of departure for a whole new history of thought and life? Therefore, the Incarnation of the Son of God is the foundation, source and model, both of a new supernatural order of existence of all men and women who draw from that mystery the grace that sanctifies and saves them, and of a Christian anthropology which views each man and woman as a person, placed at the centre of society and, it may be said, of the entire world.[30]

This explains the quite specific sense in which Christology is the key to anthropology. The doctrine of Chalcedon and the other councils of the Patristic era not only presupposes rational anthropology (e.g. the truth that man is composed of material body and rational soul), it also develops and completes it by opening up the uniqueness of the personal order of existence. Personalist philosophers – whether or not, like Karol Wojtyla, they are Christians – are indebted to the Fathers of the undivided Church.

A Dramatic Anthropology
The invitation to man in *Redemptor Hominis* to 'find himself' in Christ is the expression of what I should like to call the Pope's

---

[28] See Yves Floucat, *Pour une philosophie Chrétienne. Éléments d'un débat fondamental* (Paris, 1981), pp. 43ff.

[29] Cited in H. de Lubac, *La Foi Chrétienne. Essai sur la structure du Symbole des Apôtres*, 2nd ed. (Paris, 1970), pp. 43ff.

[30] 23/3/88; *Catechesi* 7, p. 148. See the similar comments of the leading exponent of Lublin Thomism, M. A. Krapiec, *I-Man: An Outline of Philosophical Anthropology*, ET (New Britain, 1983), p. 315f.

'dramatic anthropology'. It is strikingly similar to the doctrine of 'theological person' in Balthasar's *Theodramatik*. It may be helpful once again to read the Polish Pope with the aid of the Swiss priest.

Karol Wojtyla is a dramatist.[31] His theatrical activities as performer and playwright, which pre-date his academic career by many years (he was already a back-stage errand boy at the age of eight), have left an indelible mark on his philosophical and theological writing. The concept of 'the acting person' is a dramatic one. It is as much the fruit of the Pope's experiences on stage as the product of his philosophical reflections. Wojtyla sees the human subject not as an isolated, motionless sculpture, but as an actor, in action and interaction with the other *dramatis personae*. Now the drama of human history is not produced on a merely horizontal platform. It is a 'theo-drama', God's play, in which we are cast with and by Him as His fellow actors, as partners in an interplay of divine and human freedom. Its central act, to which both prelude and *Endspiel* point, is the Incarnation, when, as the Pope says, 'God entered the history of humanity and, as a man, became an actor in that history, one of the thousands of millions of human beings but at the same time Unique!'[32] God the Son comes down from Heaven to the earthly stage, assumes human nature and a human will, in order, by His obedience unto death on the Cross, to transfigure finite freedom from within and usher it into the boundless space of divine freedom, the glorious liberty of the children of God.

According to Balthasar, for a human person to be fulfilled he has to accept the role (mission) in which God has cast him and play it with his whole being. To be a 'theological person' is to participate, like Mary and with her help, in the mission of the Son, to be sent as He is sent. In the Trinitarian person of the incarnate Word role/mission and person are identical, by an identity given *a priori* in the hypostatic union. In human persons the identity is established *a posteriori* in a lifetime of struggle, in the power of Christ, against all the

---

[31] See Karol Wojtyla, *The Collected Plays and Writings on Theater*, ET (Berkeley, 1987), *passim*.
[32] RH 1, 258.

obstructions placed by concupiscence in the way of self-giving love.[33] I discover who I am when I say Yes to my place in the Body of Christ. Paradoxically, self-fulfilment comes only through self-oblation in union with the incarnate Son, the replacement of egocentricity by Christocentricity, of self-will by obedience. 'It is no longer I who live, but Christ who lives in me, and the life I now live in the flesh I live by faith in the Son of God' (Gal. 2.20). My personhood is not a sealed-off entity, independent of my vocation and mission. No man is more truly himself than when, for love of Christ, he surrenders himself to his mission in the Church. 'Simon has to become Peter, to see himself as Peter, as the one predestined, chosen, called and finally sent by God'.[34]

When a human subject becomes in Christ a 'theological person' with a unique call and mission, he is, says Balthasar, 'de-privatized, socialized, and made the location and bearer of communion'.[35] He is an ecclesial, truly Catholic person, sharing in some sense in the 'concrete universality' of his Head. When we are baptized, Christ breaks down the prison walls of self-centredness ('our old self was crucified with Him', Rom. 6.6), and leads us into the open space of the Communion of Saints. And when in the Mass we offer His Sacrifice and receive His Body and Blood, He takes us even more deeply into 'ecstatic', self-giving existence in the likeness of the Trinity.

This, so it seems to me, is what the Pope means when he urges human persons to 'discover' themselves in Christ. He is placing us with the Eleven in the presence of the risen Jesus and inviting us to receive from His pierced hands the gift of a unique mission (cf. John 20.20, 21). The voyage of self-discovery is not a journey into ourselves, as Gnosticism and German Idealism and the many modern psychologized forms of spirituality maintain. To find our true selves we have to let go of ourselves and 'enter into Christ', assimilating in the Sacraments 'the whole reality of the Incarnation and the Redemption', passing through Jesus' wounded side to reach His Sacred Heart. He, not I, must be my centre. All that

[33] Cf. TD 2/2, p. 190.
[34] Ibid., p. 248.
[35] Ibid., p. 249.

is central to Him – the glory of the Father and the salvation of mankind – must become my inner core.

A Christocentric Understanding of Human Suffering

Only in the light of the incarnate Word, says Pope John Paul with the Second Vatican Council, can we understand man. Only in Christ, teach Pope and Council, can we understand the suffering of man:

> Through Christ and in Christ, light is shed on the riddle (*aenigma*) of sorrow and death. Apart from His Gospel, it overwhelms us.[36]

In 1983, during the Jubilee of the Cross, Pope John Paul, in all his teaching of that year but especially in the Apostolic Letter *Salvifici Doloris*, re-presented Christ as 'the only answer to man's dramatic questions concerning pain and death'. *Christ is the answer*. Jesus gives meaning to what without Him is absurd, an intractable enigma. He answers not just by His teaching, but by His own suffering.[37] He answers from the Cross.

All his life Karol Wojtyla has struggled with the problem of pain. As a child he lost his mother and only brother. During World War II, he saw his country become the scene of horrors without parallel in history. At the age of nineteen, only weeks after the Nazi invasion of Poland, he completed a verse drama – 'Greek in form, Christian in spirit' – on Job, in which the sufferer discovers the positive meaning of his pain through a vision of the Cross received by the Prophet Elihu.[38] *Salvifici Doloris* was written while he was still recovering his health after the attack on his life in 1981.

Christianity is the only religion that offers a way *through* rather than round suffering, but then only Christianity believes in One who, without ceasing to be impassible God, was made passible man. Of course, as Balthasar says, in no sense does our religion love suffering for its own sake. 'It is in solidarity with those who try to alleviate it wherever possible. But it does not

---

[36] GS 22, quoted in DS 31, 249.
[37] SD 18, 26; 222, 240.
[38] Karol Wojtyla, *The Collected Plays and Writings on Theater*, ET (Berkeley, 1987), pp. 19–74.

stop where human beings can do no more'.[39] In and through Christ humanly hopeless suffering, even death, can have a positive meaning. And what gives meaning, what transfigures the vast bulk of our woe, is not the human suffering of a human person, a mere man suffering alongside us, but the human suffering of a divine person, God-made-man suffering for us, taking our whole hideous burden upon Himself.

The Passion, says Pope John Paul, is the suffering of the man who is the only-begotten Son, and so it has 'a unique and incomparable depth and intensity', 'pervading, redeeming, and ennobling' all human suffering. The Holy Father, like all the Church's theologians from Irenaeus to Thomas and Balthasar, maintains that the Incarnate Son of God suffered the greatest pain endured or endurable by a human being. Somehow, as humanity's Head, in His real human sufferings of body and soul, He touched and embraced the agony of every man. He became a 'sharer in all human suffering'. In obedience to the Father, loving us to the very end, He took on all our guilt and so took in all our pain. He bore our sins and thus carried our sorrows. He was wounded for our transgressions (cf. Isa. 53.4ff.).[40] As Balthasar says, by taking upon Himself 'our guilt and thus the real cause of our sorrows and hopelessness', He opened up for us 'unbounded joy'.

The crucified and risen Christ does not simply alter our thinking about suffering. He is more than an example for us. By His Passion all pain is objectively and in principle changed. When I come to suffer, says the Pope, I find that my suffering is in a new situation, 'a completely new dimension and a new order'. It has been made His own by the Son of God and offered up, in loving obedience, to His Father for the supreme good of the world's redemption.[41] As Jacques Maritain said, 'Christ suffered our sufferings before us, and He put into them together with grace and charity, a salvific power and the seed of transfiguration. Thus human suffering is not abolished, because

---

[39] 'Freude inmitten der Angst', *Du krönst das Jahr mit deiner Huld. Radiopredigten* (Einsiedeln, 1982), p. 26.

[40] SD 17–20, 219–228; 19/10/88, *Catechesi 9*, p. 22f.; *Du krönst das Jahr mit deiner Huld*, p. 27.

[41] Ibid., 18, 224.

men, by the blood of Christ and the merits of Christ in which they participate, are with Him the co-authors of their salvation.'[42]

To 'share Christ's sufferings' in the Pauline sense (cf. Phil. 3.10) means, first of all, through faith to discover that my sufferings are already Christ's and therefore 'enriched with a new content and meaning', and secondly in charity to unite my sufferings to His Sacrifice for the glory of God and for our own and our brethren's salvation.[43] Fellowship in Christ's afflictions is the only way to hear His answer to the question of suffering. Christ replies by calling:

> Christ does not explain the abstract reasons for suffering, but before all else He says: 'Follow me!, Come! Take part through your suffering in this work of saving the world, a salvation achieved through my suffering! Through my Cross.'[44]

We can now see what St Paul means when he speaks of 'making up what is lacking in Christ's sufferings' (Col. 1.24). Nothing is lacking in the Head. He died saying, 'It is accomplished' (John 19.30). His sufferings were super-abundant, infinite in their merit and saving power. He reigns now in glory, and death has no dominion over Him. But much is still lacking in His members; they must be conformed to their Head, unite their sufferings to His. As St Augustine says, 'Christ is still suffering, not in His own flesh, which He took with Him into heaven, but in my flesh, which is still suffering on earth'.[45] The Pope expounds the mystery in similar fashion:

> The suffering of Christ created the good of the world's redemption. This good in itself is inexhaustible and infinite. No man can add anything to it. But at the same time, in the mystery of the Church as His Body, Christ has in a sense opened His own redemptive suffering to all human suffering. In so far as man becomes a sharer in Christ's sufferings . . . to that extent he in his own way completes the suffering through which Christ accomplished the Redemption of the world.[46]

[42] De la grâce et de l'humanité de Jésus (Paris, 1967), p. 44f.
[43] SD 20, 227.
[44] Ibid., 26, 241.
[45] Enarrationes in Psalmos 142; PL 137. 1846.
[46] SD 24, 233.

Our Head wants us to co-operate in the most beautiful of His works, the salvation of our race. In a way we shall never understand in this life, in the Mystical Body, in the Communion of Saints, the sufferings of one member, when offered up in love, can be of benefit to another. It was St Paul's daily experience. 'If we are afflicted, it is for your comfort and salvation' (2 Cor. 1.5).

The Church's 'making up' of what is 'lacking' derives its efficacy from Christ's Cross and Resurrection. It is by the grace of the Head that the Body can collaborate. It is through His fullness, not because of any flaw, that a place is reserved for us in the work of redemption. The risen Christ pours the Holy Spirit through the scars of His glorified body into our hearts, so that suffering can be transformed into salvific love.[47] By thus completing what is lacking in Christ's afflictions, we do something for the Church, for our brothers and sisters:

> Suffering is, in fact, a vocation; it is a calling to accept the burden of pain in order to transform it into a sacrifice of purification and of reconciliation offered to the Father in Christ and with Christ, for one's own salvation and that of others.[48]

To suffer in loving union with Christ is to be an apostle, a missionary, an active labourer in the vineyard of the Lord.[49]

The Christian understanding of human suffering is Christocentric and therefore Marian. The Queen of Heaven brings everything down to earth, puts flesh on spirit, makes the abstract concrete. If we want to know what it means to 'share the sufferings of Christ', to unite our little pain to His great pain, then we look at the Woman at the foot of the Cross, uniting herself 'with a maternal heart to His Sacrifice, and lovingly consenting to the immolation of this Victim which she herself had brought forth'.[50] As Balthasar has said so nobly, 'the most rigorous theology demands of us that we pray to [the Virgin of Sorrows] and beg for admission into her open heart'. Through her we come to share in 'the interior

---

[47] Ibid., 26, 239; DV 39f., 852ff.
[48] 5/6/83.
[49] 'Even the sick are sent forth as labourers in the Lord's vineyard' (CL 53; AAS 81 (1989), 499).
[50] LG 35; *Decreta*, p. 197.

space of her Son's suffering, which is almost inaccessible to us in our sinfulness'.[51]

Compassion, completing what is lacking in Christ's sufferings, has its supreme model in the Theotokos.[52] But that is not all. She is Mother to us in our anguish: through her love and intercession, we receive from her Son the grace to unite our suffering with His. He 'wishes to penetrate the soul of every sufferer through the heart of His holy Mother, the first and most exalted of the redeemed':[53]

> As though by a continuation of that motherhood which by the power of the Holy Spirit had given Him life, the dying Christ conferred upon the ever-Virgin Mary a new kind of motherhood – spiritual and universal – towards all human beings, so that every individual, during the pilgrimage of faith, might remain, together with her, closely united to Him unto the Cross, and so that every form of suffering, given fresh life by the power of this Cross, should become no longer the weakness of man but the power of God.[54]

The Christian's final word on suffering is 'resurrection'. Sores plague his body, dark engulfs his soul, but Job defies the night: 'I know that my Redeemer liveth, and in the last day I shall rise out of the earth. And I shall be clothed again with my skin, and in my flesh I shall see my God. Whom I myself shall see, and my eyes shall behold, and not another' (Job 19.25f., Douai version). In his verse drama on Job, Wojtyla offers a beautiful gloss on this well-known passage:

> He is coming – I know He lives
> He lives – the Bright One who brings light,
> who will free from my fetters,
> who will rid me of my plight.
> I see that the Redeemer lives.
> To the dry soil He will bring rain;
> in my heart I feel alive again.
> Your bright speech is locked in my soul.
> I know I will rise with Him anew,
> to see how evil He will destroy.[55]

---

[51] *The Threefold Garland*, ET (San Francisco, 1982), p. 70.
[52] SD 25, 235ff.
[53] Ibid., 26, 240.
[54] Ibid.
[55] Karol Wojtyla, *Collected Plays and Writings on Theater* (Berkeley, 1987), p. 68.

11

Life in Christ

Christocentricity has to be lived, not just discussed. If Our Lord is 'central' for us, if we believe in Him and love Him, then we must keep His commandments as transmitted faithfully by the Church (cf. John 14.23f.). Jesus must be the practical centrepoint of our lives. As Christians, as those who in Baptism have been incorporated into Christ, our actions have to conform to the Christ-centredness of our being:

> In Jesus Christ and in His Spirit, the Christian is a 'new creation', a child of God; by his actions he shows his likeness or unlikeness to the image of the Son who is the first-born among many brethren (cf. Rom. 8.29), he lives out his fidelity or infidelity to the gift of the Spirit, and he opens or closes himself to eternal life, to the communion of vision, love and happiness with God, Father, Son, and Holy Spirit.[1]

The Answer is Christ
Man, made in God's image, longs to be one with His Creator. Having fallen in Adam, he may not be conscious of this longing; he may reject all thought of being from God and for God; and yet his untiring quest for unchanging truth and abiding

[1] VS 73. Pope John Paul outlined the same argument in a series of General Audience addresses in the summer of 1983, the Holy Year of Redemption: 'The Redemption . . . has renewed man by recreating him in Christ. Upon this new being of his there must now follow a new acting . . . The grace of the Redemption restores to health and elevates the person's intellect and will, so that his freedom is enabled, by the same grace, to act with righteousness' (18/7/83, 20/7/83).

happiness proves that only in the Infinite can he find his rest and final goal.[2]

The world's religions and philosophies are so many expressions of this desire written deep in the heart of man. They are the hunger, the thirst, the question. Christianity, or rather Christ, is heavenly bread, living water, the divinely provided answer. *Christ is the answer* to all man's questions, 'the only response fully capable of satisfying the desire of the human heart'.[3] The Word made flesh is the Father's spoken answer to all man's questions, not least his yearning to know what is good and what is evil. This is the message of the historic encyclical on the foundations of morality, *Veritatis Splendor*:

> People today need to turn once again in order to receive from Him the answer to their questions about what is good and what is evil . . . Each day the Church looks to Christ with unfailing love, fully aware that the true and final answer to the problem of morality lies in Him alone.[4]

The Holy Father sees every man in the person of that young man who once asked the Lord: 'Teacher, what good must I do to have eternal life?' (Matt. 19.16).[5] Jesus does not just utter an answer to that question: He lives it. He is the Father's eternal Word, and so all that He is and does as man is eloquent, tells us the good to be done and the evil to be avoided:

> Jesus' way of acting and His words, His deeds and His precepts constitute the moral rule of Christian life. Indeed, His actions, and in particular His Passion and Death on the Cross, are the living revelation of His love for the Father and for others.[6]

The Church does not merely preach an abstract moral theory. She makes present a living person, her Spouse, who is in Himself the law she teaches. The law was given to Israel on tablets of stone. The New Law gives Himself to the Church (and to the world) in flesh taken from Mary:

---

[2] Man's desire for God is explained beautifully in the opening pages of *The Catechism of the Catholic Church* (CCC 27ff.).

[3] VS 7.

[4] Ibid., nn. 8, 85.

[5] See chapter 1 and *passim*.

[6] VS 20.

Jesus Himself is the living 'fulfilment' of the Law inasmuch as He fulfils its authentic meaning by the total gift of Himself.[7]

The Beatitudes are not a mere ideal, a Utopian dream; they are already a reality in the Lord Jesus:

These latter are above all promises, from which there also indirectly flow normative indications for the moral life. In their originality and profundity they are a sort of *self-portrait of Christ*, and for this very reason are *invitations to discipleship and to communion of life with Christ*.[8]

The moral life is nothing other than the following of Christ. He himself is the only way for us to reach our final goal, the end of all strivings: the happiness of the Father's heart:

Following Christ is thus the essential and primordial foundation of Christian morality; just as the people of Israel followed God who led them through the desert towards the Promised Land (cf. Exod. 13.21), so every disciple must follow Jesus, towards whom he is drawn by the Father Himself (cf. John 6.44).[9]

Christ the Liberator of Liberty
Man, made in God's image, is a rational creature, endowed with intellect and will. His capacity to know the truth and to will freely has not been destroyed by the sin of Adam, but it has been weakened and wounded. There is a darkness that needs to be scattered, an unruliness that cries out for order. It is, in fact, Christ the truth who enlightens man's mind and shapes his freedom so that he can reach the glorious liberty for which he was made. Freedom itself has to be set free, and it is the incarnate Son of God who brings deliverance. He 'has set us free for freedom' (cf. Gal. 5.1):[10]

Christ reveals, first and foremost, that the frank and open acceptance of truth is the condition of authentic freedom: 'You will know the truth and the truth will set you free' (John 8.32) . . . The true worshippers of God must thus worship Him 'in spirit and truth' (cf. John 4.23): in this worship they become free.

[7] Ibid., 15.
[8] Ibid., 16.
[9] Ibid., 19.
[10] Ibid., 86.

Worship of God and a relationship with truth are revealed in Jesus Christ as the deepest foundation of freedom. Furthermore, Jesus reveals by His whole life, and not only by His words, that freedom is acquired in love, that is, in the gift of self. The one who says 'Greater love has no man than this, that a man lay down his life for his friends' (John 15.13) freely goes out to meet His Passion (cf. Matt. 26.46), and in obedience to the Father gives His life on the Cross for all men (cf. Phil. 2.6–11). Contemplation of Jesus Crucified is thus the highroad which the Church must tread every day if she wishes to understand the full meaning of freedom: the gift of self in service to God and one's brethren.[11]

Man finds his fulfilment in God, who is Trinity, the mystery of self-giving love. He can only attain the splendid freedom of the Father's adopted sons if he lets himself be taken by the Holy Spirit into the self-emptying love of the Son-made-man. Liberty is liberated at the intersection of freedom and truth, that is, on the Cross.

Morality and the Grace of Christ

The incarnate Son of God is not just a teacher of morality, not a mere model for us to imitate. He is the embodiment of what He teaches and therefore the source of the life we are called to live. We do not follow at an uninvolved distance, but by 'holding fast to the very person of Jesus, partaking of His life and His destiny, sharing in His free and loving obedience to the will of the Father'.[12] Participation in Christ makes possible imitation of Christ:

> Following Christ is not an outward imitation, since it touches man at the very depths of his being. Being a follower of Christ means becoming conformed to Him who became a servant even to giving Himself on the Cross (cf. Phil. 2.5–8). Christ dwells by faith in the heart of the believer (cf. Eph. 3.17), and thus the disciple is conformed to the Lord. This is the *effect of grace*, of the active presence of the Holy Spirit in us.[13]

If, as the Pelagian heretics believed, our Saviour offered only external helps of example and instruction, then Christian

[11] Ibid., 87.
[12] Ibid., 19.
[13] Ibid., 21.

morality would be an impossible dream. But, in fact, He lavished on us an infinitely greater gift: the Holy Spirit sent from the Father to indwell our hearts and empower us for good and holy living. With the inward supernatural help of God's grace, nothing is impossible. Man cannot imitate Christ's love by his own resources, but he does become 'capable of this love by virtue of a gift received':[14]

> Temptations can be overcome, sins can be avoided, because together with the commandments the Lord gives us the possibility of keeping them . . . And if redeemed man still sins, this is not due to an imperfection of Christ's redemptive act, but to man's will not to avail himself of the grace which flows from that act. God's command is, of course, proportioned to man's capabilities; but to the capabilities of the man to whom the Holy Spirit has been given; of the man who, though he has fallen into sin, can always obtain pardon and enjoy the presence of the Holy Spirit.[15]

Christocentric Morality and the Church

Pope John Paul's Christocentricity is ecclesial: the Head is never separated from the Body, the Groom is not divorced from the Bride. It is from the Church, therefore, he tells us, that the full splendour of Christ's moral truth shines upon the world:

> Jesus Christ, the 'light of the nations', shines upon the face of His Church, which He sends forth to the whole world to proclaim the Gospel to every creature (cf. Mark 16.15). Hence the Church . . . offers to everyone the answer which comes from the truth about Jesus Christ and His Gospel.[16]

Christ is the answer to all man's questions, and it is from the Church of Christ that man receives that answer. 'Christ's relevance for people of all times is shown forth in His Body, which is the Church.'[17] In ascending to the right hand of the Father, the glorified Son has not abandoned the Church. He remains 'always present and at work in our midst'.[18] By the

[14] Ibid., 22.
[15] Ibid., 102–103.
[16] Ibid., 2. Cf. 28, 95 and *passim*.
[17] Ibid., 25.
[18] Ibid., 25.

working of the Holy Spirit, the moral teaching He gave to the Apostles lives on in the Tradition of the Church and is expounded faithfully in each generation by the Magisterium:

> The Church, in her life and teaching, is thus revealed as 'the pillar and bulwark of the truth' (1 Tim. 3.15), including the truth regarding moral action.[19]

We have said that Jesus gives us not only moral teaching but also the power of grace by which to be faithful to that teaching. It is in the Church, through the Sacraments, that we receive the grace to follow Christ, to observe the law of God. The grace of the Holy Spirit flowing from the Saviour's wounded Heart renders us capable of that loving gift of self in which alone our freedom becomes free. The Eucharistic Sacrifice, in particular, is 'the source and power of that complete gift of self, which Jesus commands us to commemorate in liturgy and life':[20]

> It is in the saving Cross of Jesus, in the gift of the Holy Spirit, in the Sacraments which flow from the pierced side of the Redeemer, that believers find the grace and the strength always to keep God's holy law, even amid the gravest of hardships.[21]

Christology and the Confusion in Moral Theology
In defending the Church's moral teaching, Pope John Paul II is guarding the realism of the Incarnation. The confused and confusing moral theologies of our time turn out to have Christological error at their root. For example, the charges of 'physicalism' levelled at the Church's understanding of Natural Law are symptoms of a lofty angelism, a view of man in which the human body is 'a raw datum, devoid of any meaning and moral values until freedom has shaped it in accordance with its design'.[22] Now one who looks on man as an angel has not fully grasped the truth of God-made-man, God in flesh and blood.

The denial that there is such a thing as an intrinsically evil act is also a Christological error. The refusal to accept that the Church can teach particular norms with universal and un-

---

[19] Ibid., 27.
[20] Ibid., 21.
[21] Ibid., 103.
[22] Ibid., 48. See p. xvif. above.

changing force strikes against both the particularity and the universality of the incarnate Word and Redeemer:

By becoming incarnate, the Word entered fully into our daily existence, which consists of concrete human acts. By dying for our sins, He re-created us in the original holiness which must be expressed in our daily activity in the world.[23]

As the Fathers of Orthodoxy taught against the abstract Christology of the Iconoclasts, the divine Word assumed into the unity of the divine person a complete *and concrete* human nature, not a mere 'general idea' of humanness, and He merited our salvation by specific historical human acts. In becoming man, He entered into human relationships both universal (He united Himself somehow, as Head, with every man) and particular (He became the Child of the Virgin Mary of Nazareth). Now that He is in glory at the right hand of the Father, His human words and actions on earth live on, in the Sacraments and teaching of the Church, with a sanctifying and normative force that is inseparably universal and concrete, applicable to all men at all times and in all places, and to all their specific acts. St Gregory Nazianzen says of the incarnate Word that 'He bears me wholly within Himself, with my weaknesses, in order to consume in Himself what is evil'.[24] How could that be true if He did not, through His Church, give me not only grace to heal the weakness of my will, but also certain knowledge, with respect to specific actions, of what is good and what is evil? To claim that the Church proposed only moral 'ideals' which then have to be adapted to the 'concrete possibilities of man' ignores the fact it is 'only in the mystery of Christ's Redemption' that 'we discover the "concrete" possibilities of man'.[25]

The Church, says Pope John Paul, 'does not simply present "ideals"', platitudes, vague generalities:

Rather she teaches *who* man is, created by God in Christ, and therefore what his true good is. The moral law is not something extrinsic to the person: it is the very human person himself in so

[23] 12/11/88.
[24] *Oratio* 30, 6; PG 36. 109.
[25] VS 103.

far as he is called *in* and *by* the creative act itself to be and to fulfil himself freely in Christ.[26]

The Church's moral teaching is concrete because human nature exists only *in concreto*, in definite subjects. It is 'man most concrete' – every human being 'from the moment he is conceived beneath his mother's heart' – who is redeemed in Jesus Christ, whom Balthasar calls the *universale concretum et personale*, the personal 'concrete universal'.[27]

The Church's moral teaching is not only particular in the sense that it bears upon specific actions, but also universal in the sense that it insists that there are certain specific actions which are *always and everywhere* gravely wrong because of their object. The immutability of these norms has its source in the changelessness of Christ:

> 'The Church affirms that underlying so many changes there are some things which do not change and are ultimately founded upon Christ, who is the same yesterday and today and for ever.' Christ is the 'Beginning' who, having taken on human nature, definitively illumines it in its constitutive elements and in its dynamism of charity towards God and neighbour.[28]

Natural and Revealed Law United in Christ

The Christocentricity of the Pope's moral teaching does not involve any neglect of Natural Law ethics. Theological ethical reflection, centred on Christ, builds on and completes rational ethical reflection:

> The creative Wisdom that is the measure of all reality, in the Truth of which every creature is true, has a name: the incarnate Word, the Lord Jesus dead and risen. In Him and in view of Him man is created, because the Father – in His utterly free plan – has wanted man to participate in the only-begotten Son in the Trinitarian life itself. And therefore only theological ethics can give an *entirely* true response to the moral questioning of man.[29]

---

[26] 10/4/86.
[27] See Hans Urs von Balthasar, *A Theology of History*, ET (London & Sydney, 1970), p. 89, and my own book, *The Mysteries of March. Hans Urs von Balthasar on the Incarnation and Easter* (London, 1990), p. xixf.
[28] VS 53.
[29] 10/4/86.

This is an extraordinarily rich statement, opening up new possibilities for the theological understanding of Natural Law.

Following St Augustine, St Thomas teaches that the Eternal Law can be appropriated in a special way to the Second Person of the Blessed Trinity, the Father's consubstantial Word and Wisdom, in whom the Father expresses not only Himself but creatures as well.[30] Human nature, created by God, bears the special imprint of His Wisdom, who is also His Law; the Natural Law is, in fact, none other than the participation of Eternal Law in the rational creature.[31] Now when the Son assumes human nature in the womb of the Virgin, image meets archetype. Eternal Law is not simply inscribed into a human heart, He actually has a human mind and heart of His own, a mind with unique human knowledge of the Father's will and a heart perfectly obedient to it. Christ, who is divine revelation in His very person, in His actions as well as His words, completes and elevates Natural Law, and entrusts it thus restored to His Church. In all that He is as man – in the womb of Mary and the manger in Bethlehem, sawing timber in Nazareth and nailed to the tree on Calvary – the incarnate Word reveals the Father's love and fulfils His law.[32] This is at least part of what Pope Leo XIII meant when he said that 'the natural precepts of morality and the ancient law' were 'perfected and crowned by [Christ's] declaration, explanation and sanction'.[33]

Summarizing *Veritatis Splendor*, Massimo Serretti has written:

> *Veritatis Splendor* confirms with indisputable clarity that Jesus Christ is our law. In His person all the demands of the Father found an affirmative response ... There is no natural law that does not have its root in Him: 'All things were made through

[30] Cf. ST 1a2ae 93, 1, ad 2; 93, 4, ad 2; 93, 6, ad 1. Cf. VS 43.

[31] Cf. ST 1a2ae 91, 2; 96, 2, ad 1; 97, 1, ad 1. 'Reason draws its own truth and authority from the Eternal Law, which is none other than Divine Wisdom Itself' (VS 40).

[32] See my book *Redeemer in the Womb*. Jesus Living in Mary (San Francisco, 1993), pp. 147ff.

[33] *Tametsi Futura Prospicientibus* AAS 33 (1900–1901), 279; *The Papal Encyclicals* (1878–1903) (New York, 1981), p. 474.

Him, and without Him was not anything made that was made' (John 1.3; cf. Col. 1.16). He is the 'centre of the cosmos and of history', the keystone of the universe.[34]

A New Chorus of Christocentric Voices

The Fathers of the Second Vatican Council called for a renewed, more truly Christ-centred moral theology.[35] Pope John Paul II has responded to that call throughout his pontificate, especially in *Veritatis Splendor*, as have other scholars who work in this field in a spirit of Catholic fidelity. For example, Hans Urs von Balthasar, in his 'Nine Propositions on Christian Ethics', written originally for the International Theological Commission, presents the incarnate Son in all the mysteries of His life as 'the fulfilled concrete normal of all ethical actions'.[36] 'He is and lives the "new commandment".'[37] Similarly, Carlo Caffara presents the moral norm as 'fundamentally only one', namely 'the words, life, and death of Jesus', and says that 'the believer's action . . . must conform to his being-in-Christ'.[38] Finally, Germain Grisez has written, or rather is writing, *The Way of the Lord Jesus* in conscious and deliberate response to the Council's call. He observes, rightly in my opinion, that 'too much of what has been published in recent years, far from being centred upon Jesus, is vitiated by substantial compromises with secular humanism'.[39] True Christ-centredness, as we discover it in the teaching of Pope John Paul II, is Trinitarian, Marian, ecclesial, and sacramental. It is pleasing to note these same characteristics in the Christocentric moral theologies of our time.

[34] 'L'uomo tra l'immagine di Dio e gli idoli dell'autoconoscenza', *La Nuova Europa* (1994), 26.

[35] 'Other theological disciplines should also be renewed by livelier contact with the mystery of Christ and the history of salvation. Special attention needs to be given to the development of moral theology' (OT 16; *Decreta*, p. 377f.).

[36] *The International Theological Commission: Texts and Documents (1969–1985)* (San Francisco, 1989), pp. 108ff.

[37] *Theologik* 2 (Einsiedeln, 1985), p. 273. See M. Ouellet, 'The Foundation of Christian Ethics according to Hans Urs von Balthasar', *Communio* 17 (1990), 379–401.

[38] *Living in Christ: Fundamental Principles of Catholic Moral Teaching*, ET (San Francisco, 1987), p. 65.

[39] *The Way of the Lord Jesus*, vol. 1, Christian Moral Principles (Chicago, 1983), p. xxx.

12

The Mission of
Christ the Redeemer

On 7 December 1990, Pope John Paul II gave the Church another radically Christocentric document, this time, on the twenty-fifth anniversary of the conciliar decree *Ad Gentes*, an encyclical letter on the permanent validity of the Church's missionary mandate: *Redemptoris Missio*. All the familiar motifs are discernible. The title itself is eloquent; the Church has been entrusted with the very 'mission of Christ the Redeemer'. In the opening paragraphs, the cry that echoed through St Peter's Square on 22 October 1978 resounds with new drama: 'Peoples everywhere, open the doors to Christ!'[1] The Christ-centred message of *Redemptor Hominis* ('the programme of my pontificate') is re-issued: the Church's 'fundamental function', always but especially now, is to direct the gaze of all mankind towards Jesus Christ, in whom alone authentic liberation can be found, in whom alone man can understand himself.[2] The Pope is speaking *ad intra* to his 'venerable brothers' and 'beloved sons and daughters', but his intention is to turn them *ad extra*, to that vast number of people who do not know Christ and do not belong to the Church. 'When we consider this immense portion of humanity which is loved by the Father and for whom He sent His Son, the urgency of the Church's mission is obvious'.[3]

[1] Rmi 3.
[2] Ibid., 4; cf. 2.
[3] Ibid., 3.

101

The End of Hesitation
The Holy Father looks on mission as on everything else with
the realism of faith and hope, inclining to neither facile
optimism nor naive pessimism. He acknowledges light and
shadows, hints of springtime as well as sure signs of fall. In the
last twenty-five years local churches have expanded, the laity
have become more involved in evangelization, and dialogue
with other religions proceeds apace. But there is also hesitation,
a failure of nerve, a tragic waning of missionary activity
directed specifically *ad gentes*, to the non-Christian peoples of
the world. The Pope's intentions in *Redemptoris Missio* are
correspondingly twofold. His chief aim is to invite the Church
to renew her commitment to proclaim the Gospel to all the
nations, 'for missionary activity renews the Church, revitalizes
faith and Christian identity, and offers fresh enthusiasm and
new incentive'.[4] But to achieve this positive goal it is necessary
to 'clear up doubts and ambiguities regarding missionary
activity *ad gentes*'.[5] Errors have to be refuted, confusions
dispelled, hesitations overcome. Some of these derive from an
unnuanced understanding of the Church's 'missionary nature'.
True, the Church is always and everywhere missionary.
True, some traditionally Christian areas are in need of re-
evangelization. Nevertheless, there is still a specific and
imperative need for the mission to non-Christian nations.[6]

On close examination, most 'doubts and ambiguities' about
mission turn out to be Christological and ecclesiological.
What more than anything else has weakened the Church's
'missionary thrust towards non-Christians'[7] has been the
denial or compromise of the absolute uniqueness of Jesus Christ
and His Church. For example, with regard to the Kingdom
of God, some hold the opinion that mission should be
'Kingdom-centred', aimed at helping people to be 'more
human' and to build a more just world, rather than 'Church-
centred', aimed at helping them towards conversion and
Baptism. The suggestion is made that the Kingdom should be

[4] Ibid., 2.
[5] Ibid.
[6] Ibid., 32–33.
[7] Ibid., 2.

presented theocentrically rather than Christocentrically in order to find 'common ground' with other religions.[8] We should not strive, some say, to bring non-Christians to explicit faith in Jesus Christ and membership of His Church, but rather encourage them to practise their native religions with more dedication.[9] The Second Vatican Council cannot be blamed as the source of such erroneous opinions; on the contrary, they frustrate its most fundamental aspiration. Vatican II has not been tried and found wanting, the Holy Father seems to be saying, it has still not been tried.[10]

The Uniqueness of Jesus Christ

The Pope begins the first movement of his encyclical-symphony, in the style of Bruckner, with a series of thunderous chords re-affirming the absolute uniqueness of Jesus Christ. He is the only way to the Father, the sole Saviour of all, the unique revealer of the Triune God, the one mediator between God and man. This is the major theme; every subsequent bar re-echoes its melody. The Church's mission to all mankind is born of faith in the incomparable Christ.[11]

Jesus Christ is the only Saviour. Salvation is in no one else and by no other name (cf. Acts 4.10, 12). If a human being is saved, it is in the blood of the Lamb. Jesus Christ is 'the only one able to reveal God and lead to God'.[12] Indeed, in His very person, He is 'the definitive self-revelation of God'. In His Son-made-man, the Father has made Himself known in the fullest possible way. St Bonaventure and St John of the Cross agree: He is the All of the Father.[13] This is why the Church is universal of her very nature: 'She cannot do other than proclaim the Gospel, that is, the fullness of the truth which God has enabled us to know

[8] Ibid., 17.
[9] Ibid., 46.
[10] Cf. 19 (on the Christocentricity of Vatican II and Pope Paul VI).
[11] Ibid., 4.
[12] Ibid., 5. See Crossing the Threshold of Hope (New York, 1994), p. 45f.
[13] In giving us His Son, the Father 'gave us all He was, all He had, all He could' (St Bonaventure, Vigilia Nativitatis Domini, Sermo 1; Quaracchi IX, 89A). 'In giving us His Son, His only Word (for He possesses no other), He spoke everything to us at once in this sole Word – and He has no more to say' (St John of the Cross, The Ascent of Mount Carmel 2, 22; Collected Works, ET, K. Kavanaugh OCD and O. Rodriguez OCD (Washington, 1979), p. 179.

about Himself'.[14] *And Jesus Christ is the one mediator between God and man* (cf. 1 Tim. 2.5–7). 'No one . . . can enter into communion with God except through Christ by the working of the Holy Spirit.'[15] Now if we believe that Christ is the one Saviour of all, it follows that the Church, His Bride and co-worker, has the mission of proclaiming Him to all.[16] Indeed, He is the very Good News she preaches.[17] Without Him she has nothing to offer the world:

> Just as the whole economy of salvation has its centre in Christ, so too all missionary activity is directed to the proclamation of His mystery. The subject of proclamation is Christ who was crucified, dead, and is risen; through Him is accomplished our full and authentic liberation from evil, sin and death; through Him God bestows 'new life' that is divine and eternal.[18]

The Church's missionary proclamation has as its end conversion, that gift and work of the Blessed Trinity by which a person is moved to open his heart to believe in and confess the Lord Jesus Christ.[19] And conversion, by the will of Christ, is joined to Baptism, which is not just an external attestation of conversion, but 'the sacrament which signifies and effects rebirth from the Spirit, establishes real and unbreakable bonds with the Blessed Trinity, and makes us members of the Body of Christ, which is the Church'.[20] To those who refuse to address the call to conversion and Baptism to non-Christians, saying it is enough to help them become 'more human or faithful to their own religion', the Pope says that they overlook the truth 'that every person has the right to hear the Good News of the God who reveals and gives Himself in Christ, so that each one can live out in its fullness his or her proper calling'.[21]

The proclamation of Christ must be accompanied by a missionary spirituality of intimate communion with Christ, a

[14] Rmi 5.
[15] Ibid.
[16] Ibid., 9.
[17] Ibid., 13.
[18] Ibid., 44.
[19] Ibid., 46.
[20] Ibid., 47.
[21] Ibid., 46.

sharing in His self-emptying love.[22] The whole point of mission is 'to enable people to share in the communion which exists between the Father and the Son'.[23] We are missionaries because of what we are, as the Church that partakes of the Trinity's life of love, before we become missionaries in word and deed. That is why the saint, living in wholehearted friendship with Jesus and His Father in the Holy Spirit, is the first and most effective missionary.[24] The holy man or woman lets Jesus shine through. 'What we preach is not ourselves, but Jesus Christ as Lord, with ourselves as your servants for Jesus' sake' (2 Cor. 4.5). Only a lived Christocentricity, a convergence of person and mission, can draw men to the Church.

The Trinitarian Christocentricity of the Church's Mission
The missionary nature of the Church is based on the Trinitarian missions,[25] the sending of the Son by the Father, the sending of the Spirit by the Father and the Son. The Church continues and co-operates with the mission of the Son, and she does so in and by the Holy Spirit. Christ sends the Apostles in the Spirit, just as He was sent by the Father.[26]

The Spirit is present and active in a special way in the Church, but also universally, in every time and place. He is at work in the heart of every man through the 'seeds of the Word' in the diversity of human cultures.[27] But this universally active Spirit, the Pope stresses, is the Spirit of Jesus and the Soul of His Mystical Body; He is not an 'alternative to Christ'. Whatever He achieves in human hearts outside of Christendom is a 'preparation for the Gospel and can only be understood in reference to Christ, the Word who took flesh by the power of the Spirit'. The Spirit blows where He wills, but where He wills to blow is towards the Son of the Virgin Mary in His Church. 'The universal activity of the Spirit is not to be separated from His particular activity within the Body of Christ, which is the

[22] Ibid., 8.
[23] Ibid., 23.
[24] Ibid., 90.
[25] Ibid., 1.
[26] Ibid., 22.
[27] Ibid., 28. See also *Crossing the Threshold of Hope* (New York, 1994), p. 81.

Church.'[28] Indeed, His universal activity cannot even be discerned without the Christ-centred eyes of faith. The particular provides us with our only entry to the universal Moderate realism – the universal *existo in re* – is the only realism.

What I called above the 'Christocentric Pneumatology' of Pope John Paul is an implicit rejoinder and valuable corrective to the opinions of Karl Rahner, who inverts the order of the divine missions by proceeding from a 'universal Pneumatology' towards Christology. Since, on Rahner's view, God has already communicated Himself transcendentally to all mankind in the Spirit (the 'supernatural existential'), Jesus Christ becomes simply the 'unsurpassable apex' or sacramental seal of a 'universal history of grace'. By contrast, in *Redemptoris Missio*, but especially in *Dominum et Vivificantem*, John Paul shows how the universally active Spirit is inseparable from the water and the blood (cf. 1 John 5.8); He does not flow from some indeterminate source, but from the pierced heart of the Redeemer.[29]

The Christocentric Kingdom
The Pope leaves his readers in no doubt: the missiological doctrine described above of a 'Kingdom of God' without connection with the incarnate Word and His Body–Bride 'is not the Kingdom of God as we know it from revelation'. The Kingdom has its centre in Christ:

> The Kingdom of God is not a concept, a doctrine, or a programme subject to free interpretation, but is before all else a person with the face and name of Jesus of Nazareth, the image of the invisible God. If the Kingdom is separated from Jesus, it is no longer the Kingdom of God which He revealed.[30]

A Kingdom separated from Jesus is a mere ideological Utopia, an impersonal and anti-human collective. By contrast, the true

---

[28] Ibid., 29.
[29] 'It is permissible', says Rahner, 'to proceed from a universal Pneumatology to a Christology, and not merely to move conversely. In this perspective Jesus Christ appears as the unsurpassable apex of a universal history of grace grounded on God's self-communication to the world as a whole' (*Schriften zur Theologie* 14, p. 56).
[30] Rmi 18.

Kingdom of God and His Christ is a communion with God and among men in which the human person is ennobled and his freedom not crushed but enriched:

The Kingdom is inseparable from the Body as well as from the Head:

> It is true that the Church is not an end unto herself, since she is ordered towards the Kingdom of God of which she is the seed, sign and instrument. Yet, while remaining distinct from Christ and the Kingdom, the Church is indissolubly united to both. Christ endowed the Church, His body, with the fullness of the benefits and means of salvation. The Holy Spirit dwells in her, enlivens her with His gifts and charisms, guides and constantly renews her. The result is a unique and special relationship which, while not excluding the action of Christ and the Spirit outside the Church's visible boundaries, confers upon her a specific and necessary role; hence the Church's special connection with the Kingdom of God and of Christ, which she has the mission of announcing and inaugurating among all peoples.[31]

In this section of *Redemptoris Missio* strong affinities can be detected between the Pope's teaching on the Kingdom and the work of several past and present members of his International Theological Commission. For example, in an article in *Communio* in 1986, Balthasar unfolded the relationship of the Kingdom with Jesus and His Church as follows:

> Jesus, the One sent by the Father, sees Himself fundamentally as the Kingdom that is coming, but when His mission is completed, He sees Himself as the Kingdom that has truly come. The community founded by Him is, therefore, quite rightly proclaimed as the Kingdom of God, above all as the Kingdom of Christ.

Balthasar added that this identification depended on the early Church's fidelity to her missionary nature:

> She could do this as long as she saw herself as essentially missionary. She could see herself as the place in which a real coming of the Kingdom takes place – in faith, hope, love, in the Sacrament of Baptism and the celebration of the Eucharist – yet

[31] Ibid.

always in the expectation of an eschatological coming for the world as a whole. The proclamation of this coming belonged to the Church's innermost being.[32]

The duality of the Kingdom's coming in the Church – already and not yet – is most happily expressed in *Lumen Gentium*'s description of the Church as the 'germ' and 'beginning' of the Kingdom. This 'faithfully restores' the early Church's view of the Kingdom/Church relationship.

Another member of the Commission, Father Christoph Schönborn OP, sees the present-day secularization of the concept of the Kingdom as a continuation of the 'radical eschatologism' that has dominated discussion since Loisy and Schweitzer. Leonardo Boff, for example, reproduces a classically Modernist and Liberal Protestant thesis when he argues that Jesus did not want to found the Church, but to proclaim the Kingdom; the Church, he says, is a temporary 'substitute' for the Kingdom. According to Schönborn, views such as this derive from an impoverished Christology. Its proponents would do well to learn from Karl Barth, who at one stage was a 'thorough-going eschatologist', regarding the time between the Resurrection and the Parousia as an empty desert. However, he came to see, as did Balthasar, that Christian eschatology has to be Christocentric: Jesus is, was, and will be the Kingdom.[33]

Recent official documents of the International Theological Commission contain many of the ideas in the essays of two of its members. The Kingdom, according to the Commission, is indissolubly united with both Christ and His Church. Jesus 'announces' it and 'makes it present in His own person, in His actions, and in His words'. When Vatican II calls the Church the 'seed' and 'beginning' of the Kingdom, it brings out 'their simultaneous unity and difference'.[34]

---

[32] 'Gottes Reich und die Kirche', *International katholische Zeitschrift* 15 (1986), 125.

[33] Karl Barth, *Die kirchliche Dogmatik* 3/2 (Zürich, 1959), p. 589. Cf. C. Schönborn OP, 'Das Reich Gottes und die himmlisch-irdische Kirche' in *Existenz im Übergang* (Einsiedeln & Trier, 1987), 64–71.

[34] The references are respectively to the 'Select Themes of Ecclesiology' of 1985 and to the document on 'The Consciousness of Christ' (*International Theological Commission: Texts and Documents* 1969–1985 (San Francisco, 1989), pp. 303, 309).

Uniqueness and Universality

Though written before his conversion, Chesterton's *Orthodoxy* provides the best description I know of the dogmatic balance of the Catholic Church, which is neither the nervous compromise of Anglican 'comprehensiveness' nor the chaotic contradiction of Neo-Modernist 'pluralism'. It is 'the equilibrium of a man behind madly rushing horses, seeming to stoop this way and to sway that, yet in every attitude having the grace of statuary and the accuracy of arithmetic'.[35] In *Redemptoris Missio* the Holy Father provides a beautiful example of this untame central course. He asserts two sets of dynamically complementary truths: the uniqueness of Christ the Saviour and the universal availability of His saving grace; the necessity of the Church for salvation and the possibility of salvation for those who 'do not have any opportunity to come to know or accept the Gospel revelation or to enter the Church':

> It is necessary to keep these two together, namely, the real possibility of salvation in Christ for all mankind and the necessity of the Church for salvation. Both these truths help us to understand the one mystery of salvation, so that we can come to know God's mercy and our own responsibility.[36]

Salvation is offered, in a manner known only to God, to every single human being, 'not only to those who explicitly believe in Christ and have entered the Church'.[37] It cannot, however, be stressed too much that this is salvation in Jesus Christ, by His grace and through His sacrifice, and It involves a 'mysterious relationship with the Church'.[38]

[35] G. K. Chesterton, *Orthodoxy* in *Collected Works*, vol. 1 (San Francisco, 1986), p. 167f.

[36] Rmi 9.

[37] Ibid., 10.

[38] Ibid. The new Catechism re-affirms the teaching of the Fathers: 'Outside the Church there is no salvation'. It then explains what this means: 'Re-formulated positively, it means that all salvation comes from Christ the Head through the Church which is His Body' (CCC 846). Finally, it repeats the teaching of LG 16 concerning the possibility of salvation for 'those who, through no fault of their own, do not know the Gospel of Christ or His Church' (ibid., 847). See also the famous allocution *Singulari Quadam* of Pope Pius IX (DS 2865f.) and the letter of the Holy Office to the Archbishop of Boston (8 August 1949, DS 3866ff.).

Dialogue and Mission

The Pope recalls the Church to an enthusiastic mission to the non-Christian world, while at the same time explaining and defending the value of dialogue among religions. In no sense do such contacts dispense the Church from direct and explicit mission and evangelization. On the contrary, they are themselves a part of missionary activity. There is no contradiction between meeting the representatives of other religions and proclaiming Christ.[39] The Church gladly acknowledges whatever is true and holy in other religions 'as a reflection of that truth which enlightens all men'. However, 'this does not lessen her duty and resolve to proclaim without fail Jesus Christ who is "the way, the truth, and the life"'.[40] The Pope roundly condemns the relativism 'which leads to the belief that one religion is as good as another'.[41] 'Dialogue should be conducted and implemented with the conviction that the Church is the ordinary means of salvation and that she alone possesses the fullness and means of salvation.[42] Thus the meeting at Assisi in 1986, based on the Pope's conviction that 'every authentic prayer is prompted by the Holy Spirit',[43] was a bold proclamation of Christ and a witness to the unique claims of His Church. In the presence of Jews and Muslims, Hindus and Buddhists, the Holy Father humbly but firmly declared that he was 'a believer in Jesus Christ, and, in the Catholic Church, the first witness of faith in Him'.[44] Here was no syncretism, but 'dialogue-as-part-of-mission'. Never before, in the history of the world's religions, had their leaders been confronted with such an explicit proclamation of Jesus Christ. Though exploited for unsuitable ends by others, the Assisi meeting, as understood by the Holy Father, was not a blurring of Christian uniqueness, but a lucid demonstration of it. Only the Vicar of Christ could have assembled such a disparate group of men and women to pray for peace on earth.

[39] Ibid., 55.
[40] Ibid.
[41] Ibid., 36.
[42] Ibid., 55.
[43] Ibid., 2.
[44] Ibid.

We need a test, a criterion, for distinguishing respect for holiness and truth outside the Church from the hollowness of indifferentism. The test is martyrdom, 'the giving of one's life to the point of accepting death in order to bear witness to one's faith in Jesus Christ'.[45] As Balthasar shows in *Cordula*, the martyr is the model for Christian engagement in the world and a challenge to the obscuring of Christian uniqueness by such theories as Karl Rahner's 'anonymous Christianity'.[46] When he stands up and stands out for his faith, the witness reveals the transcendent newness brought into this sin-aged world by the Son of God. This is the pearl of great price, without rival or peer, and for it the martyr gives his all. In a similar way, in *Redemptoris Missio*, the Pope sees the martyr as the model missionary, '*par excellence* the herald and witness of the faith'.[47] John Paul speaks with an authority that is personal as well as official, for he has suffered physical attack for his witness to Christ's truth:

> Christian martyrs of all times – including our own – have given and continue to give their lives in order to bear witness to this faith, in the conviction that every human being needs Jesus Christ, who has conquered sin and death and reconciled mankind to God.[48]

The Church's chief missionary is not ashamed of the Gospel. 'It is the power of God for salvation to everyone who has faith' (Rom. 1.16).

---

[45] Ibid., 45.
[46] *Cordula oder der Ernstfall*, 4th ed. (Einsiedeln, 1987), *passim*.
[47] Rmi 55.
[48] Ibid., 11. On the 'witness situation' of the individual Christian, see Balthasar TD 2/2, pp. 416–419.

13

The Christ-Centred Priest

Cardinal Newman once defined a rationalist as a man who 'makes himself his own centre, not his Maker'.[1] Ever since the fall of the first man, such self-centring has afflicted human life, but since the rise of modern man, in the various forms of rationalism, it has been given a kind of intellectual respectability. It has become a philosophy, a political programme, the obsession of whole cultures. Newman finds the beginnings of rationalist egotism in the sixteenth century, when the Reformation replaced the We of Catholic communion with the I of solitary faith-experience. It was developed philosophically by Descartes and Kant, who made the knowing of the subject take precedence over the communal world of Being. It reaches a peak in our own times when the rapacious self demands a 'freedom of choice' that would destroy innocent human life. The Holy Father has no hesitation in calling this radical individualism 'a sort of practical and existential atheism':

> The individual, 'all bound up in himself ... makes himself not only the centre of his every interest, but dares to propose himself as the principle and reason of all reality'.[2]

Such a mentality can and does affect today's priest and seminarian. Bad theology, bogus spirituality, and bankrupt liturgiology entice them into subjectivism. Functionalistic theologies of ministry focus their attention on their own virtues

[1] John Henry Cardinal Newman, 'On the Introduction of Rationalistic Principles into Revealed Religion' in *Essays Critical and Historical*, vol. 1, new ed. (London, 1890), p. 33.
[2] PDV 7.

and skills. Psychologizing neo-Pelagian spiritualities offer techniques of 'self-realization'. Certain styles of liturgical celebration highlight the personality of the priest. In unholy alliance,
all these tendencies can ensnare today's priest into thinking he
must be 'his own person'.

But he is not, and he can never be. To quote the splendid
title of a book by Bishop Fulton Sheen, 'the priest is not his
own'. He belongs to Someone Else, to Christ and His Church.
His very soul bears the indelible mark of the Master's
ownership, the 'character' that conforms him to the Eternal
High Priest. When he carries out the highest deeds of his
priesthood, he acts not in his own but in Christ's person and
by His power. No priest is an island, entire of itself; he does
not draw the map of his priestly existence. Communion with
Christ, the Trinity, and the Church: that is what defines him.
As the Holy Father says in his Apostolic Exhortation on
Priestly Formation, *Pastores Dabo Vobis*, 'priestly identity' is
fundamentally 'relational':

> Through the priesthood which arises from the depths of the
> ineffable mystery of God, that is, from the love of the Father, the
> grace of Jesus Christ and the Holy Spirit's gift of unity, the priest
> sacramentally enters into communion with the bishop and with
> other priests, in order to serve the People of God who are the
> Church and to draw all mankind to Christ in accordance with the
> Lord's Prayer . . . Consequently, the nature and mission of the
> ministerial priesthood cannot be defined except through this
> multiple and rich interconnection of relationships which arise
> from the Blessed Trinity and are prolonged in the communion of
> the Church.[3]

In this chapter I want to reflect, with the help of *Pastores Dabo
Vobis*, on these 'multiple and rich' relationships, above all on
what the Holy Father identifies as the most fundamental of
them all – the priest's bond with Jesus Christ, 'the Head and
Shepherd'.[4]

[3] Ibid., 12.
[4] Ibid., 13–15. See the 1994 *Directory for the Life and Ministry of Priests*
of the Congregation for the Clergy on the Trinitarian, Christological,
Pneumatological, and Ecclesial dimensions of priestly identity (ET
(Washington, 1994), pp. 9ff.).

The Christ-Related Priest

The priest is Christ-centred, Christ-related. This has been the Holy Father's message to priests from the outset of his pontificate. To every question about priestly life and ministry, he gives the same answer: 'The priest always, and in an unchangeable way, finds the source of his identity in Christ the Priest'.[5]

Priestly Christ-relatedness must be understood correctly. First, it is sacramental, a participation in the priesthood of Him who is, as the new Catechism says, quoting St Thomas, 'the source of all priesthood'.[6] Through their Baptism, all the faithful share in Christ's priesthood,[7] but the share given to baptized males, through the 'particular' gift of the Holy Spirit in Ordination, is something different, essentially different. To the ministerial priest alone is given – in the words of *Lumen Gentium* – the 'sacred power' to 'rule the priestly people' and to 'effect the Eucharistic Sacrifice in the person of Christ'.[8] 'In the person of Christ': that is the key phrase. When we say that the priest's Christ-centredness is sacramental, we mean not only that it is brought about through a Sacrament, but also that it makes the priest himself a kind of sacrament, a sacramental sign of Christ the Priest.

Secondly, the Christ-relatedness of the priest is ontological. It establishes him in a new order of being. 'The relation of the priest to Jesus Christ, and in Him to His Church, is found in the very being of the priest, by virtue of his sacramental consecration/anointing, and in his activity, that is, in his mission or ministry.'[9] There is a 'specific ontological bond which unites the priesthood to Christ the High Priest and Shepherd'.[10] Like all the Sacraments, Holy Order is a marvel of transfiguration: by the gift of the anointing Spirit, the priest is changed and renewed in his innermost depths, converted into the likeness of Christ. The Holy Father invokes the traditional doctrine of character to explain this: the priest is 'marked permanently and

[5] *Holy Thursday Letter to Priests* (1986), n. 10.

[6] CCC 1548 (cf. ST 3a 22, 4). The ministerial priesthood is 'a participation, in the Church, in the very priesthood of Jesus Christ' (PDV 11).

[7] PDV 13.

[8] LG 10.

[9] PDV 16.

[10] Ibid., 11.

indelibly in his inner being as a minister of Jesus and of the Church'.[11]

It is important to note that, according to the Holy Father, it is through his ordination-established relationship with Christ, that the priest, as priest, relates to the Church. There is a certain 'asymmetry' about his twofold relationship with the Head and the rest of the Mystical Body. By his Baptism, he is already a member of the Body, and so, like St Augustine, he can say to his fellow Christians, 'With you I am a Christian'. However, by being configured to Christ in Ordination, he has a new ministerial relationship with them: 'For you I am a priest'. It is in and through the Bridegroom that the priest serves the Bride. The power to act in the person of the Head enables him to operate in the name of the Body. Thus the priest's relations with Christ and those he enjoys with the Church cannot be simply 'juxtaposed'. They are 'interiorly united'.[12] It is in the *communio* of the Church, through the bishop's prayer and laying on of hands, that a baptized man is brought by the Holy Spirit into a new relationship with Christ, which in turn gives him a new relationship to the bishops, his brother priests, and to the whole People of God. The priest's relation to Christ as His 'sacramental representation' is the 'basis and inspiration' for his relation to the Church.[13]

Thirdly, the priest's Christ-centredness is Trinitarian. All authentic Christ-centredness is Trinitarian, for Our Lord Jesus Christ is One of the Trinity, the incarnate Second Person, God the Son, eternally begotten of the Father in His divinity, born in time of the Blessed Virgin Mary in His humanity.

Ministerial priesthood has its source in the Triune God, in 'the love of the Father, the grace of Jesus Christ and the Holy Spirit's gift of unity'.[14] It is the fruit of the missions, the sendings, of the Son and the Spirit. The priest is 'sent forth by the Father through the mediatorship of Jesus Christ . . . in order

[11] Ibid., 70
[12] Ibid., 16.
[13] Ibid. *The Catechism of the Catholic Church* says: '. . . it is because the ministerial priesthood represents Christ that it can represent the Church' (n. 1553).
[14] PDV 12.

to live and work by the power of the Holy Spirit.[15] By the sacramental gift of the Holy Spirit, the incarnate Son gives men – first the Apostles, then bishops and priests – a share in His priestly mission from the Father. 'As the Father has sent me, even so I send you' (John 20.21).[16] The mission from the Father and the anointing by the Spirit are inseparably connected in Jesus, and so they are in His priestly servants: '. . . not only consecration but mission as well is under the seal of the Spirit and the influence of His sanctifying power'.[17] The Holy Spirit 'consecrates for mission those whom the Father calls through His Son Jesus Christ'.[18] The spiritual life of the priest is one of 'deep communion with Jesus Christ, the Good Shepherd . . . total submission of one's life to the Spirit in a filial attitude toward the Father and a trustful attachment to the Church'.[19]

The priesthood of the Son is intrinsic to His mission; His is a sacerdotal sending.[20] According to the Church Fathers, Our Lord's priestly consecration took place at the moment of His Incarnation. As St Cyril of Alexandria says, the divine Word became 'High Priest and our Apostle when He was made flesh and man like us'.[21] The Holy Virgin's womb, exclaims St Proclus of Constantinople in a homily, is 'the temple in which God became a priest'.[22] In other words, it is as man that God the Son is priest. This is the magnificent doctrine of the Epistle to the Hebrews. The Eternal High Priest is 'taken from among men and is able to sympathize with them' (Heb. 2.17f.; cf. 4.15; 5.1; 11.13). Intrinsic to the priesthood of Jesus Christ is His sacred human heart, His unique sensitivity and compassion. This has important implications for sacerdotal spirituality. If the priest is to be Christ-centred, he should be centred on Christ's own centre – the Heart whence flows every act of His priesthood. This truth did not escape the attention of the 1990 Synod, nor of

[15] Ibid.
[16] Ibid., 14.
[17] Ibid., 24.
[18] Ibid., 35.
[19] Ibid., 45, citing *Instrumentum Laboris* 30.
[20] He is sent by the Father 'as High Priest and Good Shepherd' (PDV 18).
[21] *Anathematism* 10; DS 261.
[22] *Oratio III (De Incarnatione Domini)* 3; PG 65. 708A.

the Holy Father. Spiritual formation 'can profitably make use of a proper devotion to the Sacred Heart of Jesus, one that is both strong and tender', affective without being effetely sentimental.[23] 'Priesthood', says the new Catechism, quoting St John Vianney, 'Is the love of the Heart of Jesus'.[24]

The Priest as 'Representative' of Christ

The Holy Father draws on the resources of the Tradition to unfold the riches of Christ-centred priesthood. Following the Fathers of East and West and the Scholastics of the Latin Middle Ages, what I am calling 'Christ-centredness' is defined in terms of 'sacramental representation' and 'imaging'. The priest is the 'sacramental representation of Jesus Christ, the Head and Shepherd'.[25] In 'a new and special way' the Holy Spirit 'con-figures' him to (that is, shapes him into the likeness of) Jesus Christ, the Head and Shepherd'.[26] In a certain sense, he 'imitates' Christ, 'represents the person of Christ Himself'.[27] 'The priest is a living and transparent image of Christ the Priest', the 'living image of Jesus Christ, the Spouse of the Church'.[28] He is a shepherd 'in the likeness of Jesus Christ the Good Shepherd',[29] 'a manifestation and image of the Good Shepherd'.[30] Priests are 'living instruments of Christ the Eternal Priest'.[31] They act 'in the name and in the person of Him who is Head and Shepherd of the Church'.[32] They are 'a derivation, a specific participation in and continuation of Christ Himself, the One Priest of the new and eternal covenant'.[33] As minister of 'word, sacrament, and pastoral charity', the priest shares in the tria munera Christi.[34]

[23] PDV 49.
[24] CCC 1589.
[25] PDV 15.
[26] Ibid.; cf. 21, 69, 70.
[27] Ibid., 20; cf. 57.
[28] Ibid., 12, 22; cf. 82.
[29] Ibid., 65.
[30] Ibid., 49.
[31] PO 12, cited in PDV 20.
[32] PDV 35.
[33] Ibid., 12.
[34] Cf. PDV 26. See the article by Archbishop Henryk Muszyrnski in L'Osservatore Romano (26 August 1992).

It is this sacramental representation which constitutes the essential difference between ministerial priesthood and common priesthood, as the International Theological Commission said in 1985, re-stating the teaching of *Lumen Gentium* 10, which in turn builds on Pope Pius XII's *Mediator Dei*:

> The priest acts in the name of the people precisely and only because he represents the person of our Lord Jesus Christ, considered as Head of all the members and offering Himself for them.[35]

Every one of the faithful exercises his share in Christ's priestly mission by participation in the Sacraments, by prayer, self-denial, charity, by offering up all he does and suffers in union with Christ.[36] The ministerial priest, by contrast, has the special and irreplaceable role of representing Christ, that is to say, of being the sign and instrument of Him who, in the Eucharistic Sacrifice, is principal Priest and Victim. Thus, as the Holy Father says, '"sacramental representation" of Christ serves as the basis and inspiration for the relation of the priest to the Church'.[37] By his Baptism, the priest faces the Bridegroom as a living part of the Bride. By his Ordination, he stands facing the Bride, not for his own glory, but in her service, in order to represent her beloved Spouse:[38]

> Inasmuch as he represents Christ the Head, Shepherd, and Spouse of the Church, the priest is placed not only in the Church but also facing towards (*erga*) the Church.[39]

The Priest as Icon of Christ

Throughout *Pastores Dabo Vobis* the language of representation is used interchangeably with that of imaging. The one concept illuminates the other. The priest represents Christ somewhat as an icon represents its subject. The new Catechism gives us a good working definition of what this analogy means: 'the ordained minister is as it were the "icon" of Christ

---

[35] DS 3850.
[36] Cf. LG 10.
[37] PDV 16.
[38] Ibid., 22.
[39] Ibid., 16, citing *Propositio* 7.

the Priest . . . [through him] the presence of Christ as Head of the Church is made visible in the midst of the community of believers'.[40]

The priest as icon and representation of Christ has a long and venerable history in the Tradition of the Church. Its beginnings are in the New Testament. 'He who receives anyone whom I send receives me', says Our Lord in St John's Gospel, 'and he who receives me receives Him who sent me' (John 13.20; cf. Matt. 10.40). The sending Father is received in the sent Son, because Father and Son are in each other by nature, and because the Son is the uncreated Image of the Father: 'He who has seen me has seen the Father . . . Do you not believe that I am in the Father and the Father in me?' (cf. John 14.9f.). The incarnate Son and His 'sent ones' are in each other by the grace of the Holy Spirit (cf. John 17.21f.), and so, by the logic of the Fourth Gospel, it may be concluded that the Apostles are Christ's created sacramental images. In the manner of a visible sign, He is present and active in them. St Paul repeats the teaching of the Lord. In welcoming him, he says, the Galatians received Christ Jesus Himself (cf. Gal. 4.14).

In the first years of the second century, St Ignatius of Antioch already has an iconic theology of priesthood, albeit applied to the bishop as living image of God the Father (*typos tou Patros*).[41] In the third century, St Cyprian, writing against the Aquarian heretics, who refused to use wine in the Eucharist, insists that on her altars the Church faithfully reproduces the Last Supper. The same material elements are used, and the same words of Christ are spoken by the priest. He who 'imitates what Christ then did acts in the place of Christ (*vice Christi*) and offers the true and complete sacrifice in the Church of God the Father'.[42]

According to St John Chrysostom, the priest is a 'symbol' (*symbolon*) of Christ:

[40] CCC 1142, 1549.

[41] *Epistola ad Trallianos* 3; *The Apostolic Fathers*, ed. J. B. Lightfoot, vol. 2/1 (London, 1885), p. 157f.

[42] *Epistola* 63, 14; PL 4. 397B.

The priest fulfils the role of symbol . . . Everything is God's work. He does all . . . The offering is the same, whatever the offerer is like, whether it be Paul or Peter. What Christ gave to His disciples is identical with what priests now carry out.[43]

It is during the Iconoclastic controversy that the notion of the priest as icon is more clearly defined. In his *Seven Chapters against the Iconoclasts*, St Theodore the Studite (759–826) explains why priests bless newly baptized infants with the sign of the cross rather than an icon. The reason is that the priest 'in priestly invocations' is himself the icon (*eikôn*) and imitation (*minêma*) of Christ the Mediator, and so does not require an additional material emblem for performing his liturgical functions.[44]

The theology of sacramental character, in relation to Holy Order, is expounded by the Fathers (St Gregory Nazianzen, Dionysius the Areopagite, St Maximus the Confessor) in the same iconic way. The priest is Christ's marked man, like an engraving, like a seal in wax bearing the imprint of Christ. He in turn, in the Sacrament of Baptism, is like a signet ring marking men with the imprint of adoptive sonship.[45]

The Western Scholastics develop this Patristic theology of the priest as icon. According to St Thomas, the priest is 'the figure and express form of Christ'.[46] The priest 'bears the image of Christ, in whose person and by whose power he pronounces the words of consecration . . . and so in a certain sense the Priest and Victim are the same'.[47] When he consecrates or absolves, the priest uses not his own words but the words of Christ. His I is the I of Jesus. He acts *in persona Christi*. When he offers the Sacrifice of the Mass, which renews the Sacrifice of Calvary, the priest becomes in a certain sense – representatively, iconically, instrumentally – identical with Christ. In his 'Commentary on the Sentences', St Thomas explains this mysterious identification as follows:

[43] *Homilia 2 in Epistolam Secundam ad Timotheum* 4; PG 62. 612.
[44] *Adversus Iconomachos*, cap. 4; PG 99. 493CD.
[45] *Oratio* 40, 26; PG 36. 396C.
[46] ST Supplement 34, 2.
[47] ST 83, 1, ad 3.

This Sacrament [of the Eucharist] is directly representative of the
Lord's Passion, in which Christ as Priest and Victim offered
Himself to God on the altar on the Cross. Now the Victim which
the priest offers is really the same as the one Christ offered, since
it really contains Christ. As for the minister who offers, he is not
the same in reality, but he must be the same in representation.
That is why the priest, consecrating in the person of Christ,
pronounces the words of consecration in narrative form, in the
name of Christ, so that no one may think that the Victim is
different.[48]

In its official commentary on *Inter Insigniores*, the Congregation for the Doctrine of the Faith confirms the view that the
Scholastic concept of acting *in persona Christi* is a development of
the Byzantine notion of the priest as *mimêma Christou*. It also
throws light from another angle. Priestly 'imitation' of Christ is
not only quasi-iconic, but quasi-dramatic. *Persona* here has its
classical resonance; it denotes the part played by an actor in the
Greco–Roman theatre, a part identified by the mask he wears.
According to this analogy, in the sacred drama of the liturgy, 'the
priest takes the part of Christ, lending his voice and gestures'.[49]

St Thomas strengthens the iconographic and theatrical
analogies with the concept of instrumental causality. 'Since
these words are uttered from the person of Christ, by his will
they derive from Him an instrumental power.'[50] In the Sacraments, the sacred humanity of the Word, which is the Triune
God's instrument for sanctifying us, has as its subordinate
instrument the celebrating priest and the liturgical rite. In the
Eucharist, Christ, who is the principal sacrificing priest,
employs His human instrument and image to convert bread
and wine into His Body and Blood, and thus to re-present, in an
unbloody manner, the Sacrifice of the Cross. In similar fashion,
St Bonaventure argues that the priest is a 'sign' of Christ the
Mediator, a sacrament in his very person.[51] Both he and St
Thomas stress that the priest is sign or image of Christ in his

[48] *Scriptum super librum IV Sententiarum*, d. 8, q. 2, 1, sol. 4.
[49] *The Ordination of Women*. The Official Commentary of the Sacred Congregation for the Doctrine of the Faith on its Declaration *Inter Insigniores*
(London, 1977), p. 17.
[50] ST 3a, 78, 4.
[51] *Commentarium super librum III Sententiarum*, d. 12, a. 3, q. 1.

whole person, in soul as united to body. His maleness is therefore essential to his office of being sign and image.[52]

Staretz Silouan, the great Russian Athonite monk (1866–1938), was given the extraordinary grace of insight into this mystery of the priest's imaging of Christ:

> The Lord let me see a priest – he was standing hearing confessions – in the image of Christ. Though his hair was white with age, his face looked young and beautiful . . . so inexpressibly radiant was he. In the same way I once saw a bishop during the liturgy.[53]

Like every *gratia gratis data*, this experience of Father Silouan's took place for the good of the whole Church. For our enlightenment, he was privileged to perceive in this exceptional way the ontological reality of all priesthood, its indelibly Christic character, its sacramental imaging of Jesus the Eternal High Priest.

This is the rich background to the 'iconic' theology of priesthood developed by the Holy Father in *Pastores Dabo Vobis*.

Being and Becoming the Icon of Christ

Pastores Dabo Vobis identifies two meanings of priestly Christlikeness: the 'ontological' and the 'psychological', the 'sacramental' and 'moral'; in other words, the objective and subjective.[54] By virtue of his ordination, through the indelible character conferred on him, the priest is objectively the image of Christ. However unchristlike he may be morally and spiritually, the priest is empowered to act in Christ's person, to consecrate and absolve by His power. The Sacraments he administers are efficacious *ex opere operato*, by the power of the completed rite, because Christ is working in and through him. This is a precious and consoling truth of our faith, but it should not obscure the fact that the priest is also called to be like Christ subjectively, that is to say, in heart and mind and deed. In this sense, Christlikeness is a task and a vocation to be accomplished by grace. The priest must become what he is by ordination. The

---

[52] For texts, see M. Hauke, *Women in the Priesthood?* (San Francisco, 1988), p. 454.

[53] Archimandrite Sophrony, *Wisdom from Mount Athos*. The Writings of Staretz Silouan, ET (London, 1974), p. 65.

[54] PDV 71.

Spirit of Christ assimilates a man to Christ in Ordination by conferring the character of priesthood, but the same Spirit is also given in the specific sacramental grace of Holy Order to equip the priest for the accomplishment of his ministry and the hallowing of his life. 'Yes, the Spirit of the Lord is the principal agent in our spiritual life.'[55]

> Beloved [says the Holy Father, quoting a homily to five thousand priests from throughout the world], through Ordination, you have received the same Spirit of Christ, who makes you like Him, so that you can act in His name and so that His very mind and heart might live in you. This intimate communion with the Spirit of Christ, while guaranteeing the efficacy of the sacramental actions which you perform *in persona Christi*, seeks to be expressed in fervent prayer, in integrity of life, in the pastoral charity of a ministry tirelessly spending itself for the salvation of the brethren. In a word, it calls for your personal sanctification.[56]

The iconic theology of priesthood is used by *Optatam Totius* when it sketches the foundations of spiritual formation in the seminary:

> Those who are going to be shaped into the likeness of Christ through Sacred Ordination should form the habit of drawing close to Him as friends in every detail of their lives.[57]

Pastores develops the teaching of this passage and speaks of the 'great spiritual value' of 'the search for Jesus'. If the priest is to know and love and imitate Christ, then he must look for Him where He is to be found – in *lectio divina*, in personal prayer, in the 'beauty and joy of the Sacrament of Penance', and supremely in the 'high point of Christian prayer', namely, the Eucharist.[58] These are the spiritual means by which the priest can become the icon of Christ that he is.

The holy priest, says Balthasar, is 'a man who in God has become so unimportant to himself that for him only God counts'.[59] Like the Baptist, he says, 'He must increase, but I

---

[55] Ibid., 33.
[56] Ibid.
[57] OT 8; cf. PDV 45.
[58] PDV 47–48.
[59] 'The Priest I Want', in *Elucidations*, ET (London, 1975), p. 111.

must decrease' (John 3.30). His centre of gravity, the fixed point round which his whole being turns, is Christ, Christ in His Church. There is a deep mystery in this spiritual Christ-likeness: the priest most like Christ is the priest least aware of it. He is, as the Holy Father says, a 'transparent' image of Christ. Sinful self-centring does not block out the Lord. Jesus shines through.

The Priest as Icon of Christ the Priest–Bridegroom
The priest is 'configured to', is the 'image' of, Christ as Priest–Head, Priest–Bridegroom and Priest–Shepherd. These three dimensions of Our Lord's priesthood – the capital, the spousal and the pastoral – are constantly stressed throughout the document. I should like to concentrate on the spousal. The priest, according to the Holy Father, is 'the living image of Jesus Christ, the Bridegroom of the Church'.[60]

Jesus is Priest precisely as *Sponsus Ecclesiae*. As St Paul explains in the Epistle to the Ephesians, Our Lord's supreme sacerdotal act is also husbandly: He offers Himself to the Father on the altar of the Cross for the Church, His Bride:

> Husbands, love your wives, as Christ loved the Church and gave Himself up for her (Eph. 5.25).

The man ordained to a share in Christ's priesthood partici-pates also in His Lord's husbandly relationship with the Church. He is image and instrument of the bridegroomly love of Jesus Christ:

> Of course, he will remain a member of the community as a believer alongside his other brothers and sisters who have been called by the Spirit, but in virtue of his configuration to Christ, the Head and Shepherd, the priest stands in this spousal relationship with regard to the community.[61]

This is revealed most distinctly in the central function of priestly ministry. The Holy Eucharist, says the Holy Father, 'represents, makes once again present, the sacrifice of the Cross, the full gift of Christ to the Church, the gift of His Body given and His Blood shed, as the supreme witness of the fact that He

[60] PDV 22.
[61] Ibid., 22.

is Head and Shepherd, Servant and Spouse of the Church'.[62] The Mass is a matrimonial mystery. As Pope John Paul teaches in *Mulieris Dignitatem*, 'It is the Sacrament of the Bridegroom and of the Bride. The Eucharist makes present and realizes anew in a sacramental manner the redemptive act of Christ ... It is the Eucharist above all that expresses the redemptive act of Christ the Bridegroom towards the Church His Bride'.[63]

This remarkable theology of the priesthood, at once spousal and iconic, has a direct bearing on two important questions of our times: the absolute necessity of the maleness of the priesthood and the relative necessity of priestly celibacy. The first has been well treated by the Holy Father elsewhere.[64] The reasoning can be summarized briefly here. Since Christ is Priest as Bridegroom and Bridegroom as Priest, His maleness is an essential part of His redemptive mission. It follows that those who are His sacramental representatives and icons must also be male, if there is to be that 'natural resemblance' proper to sacramental signification. This is of the very essence of the Sacrament of Holy Order as willed and instituted by Jesus Christ. For this reason, the Church insists that she does not have the power to admit women to the priesthood. Women's ordination is not simply undesirable or inexpedient; as the new Catechism firmly states, it is impossible.[65] 'A woman cannot receive the Sacrament of Order, and therefore cannot fulfil the proper function of the ministerial priesthood.'[66]

It is the relevance of the spousal and iconic theology of priesthood to celibacy which most preoccupies the Holy Father in *Pastores Dabo Vobis*. In my opinion, he presents here the profoundest exposition of the relative necessity of celibacy ever offered by the Papal Magisterium.

The argument has the power of simplicity. As the icon of Christ the Priest–Bridegroom, the priest is called, like Christ, to direct his pastoral charity, his sincere gift of self, towards the

[62] Ibid., 23.
[63] Ibid., 26.
[64] Cf. MD 26, CL 51 and the Apostolic Letter *Ordinatio Sacerdotalis* (1994), *passim*.
[65] CCC, n. 1577.
[66] CL 51.

Church. Like Christ and with the help of His grace, he must 'love the Church and give himself up for her'.[67] This spousal love of the priest for the Church is ultimately Christ-centred; it is for the love of Jesus that he loves the Church:

> The gift of self to the Church concerns her in so far as she is the Body and Bride of Jesus Christ. In this way the primary point of reference of the priest's charity is Jesus Christ Himself. Only in loving and serving Christ the Head and Spouse will charity become a source, criterion, measure and impetus for the priest's love and service to the Church, the Body and Spouse of Christ.[68]

The priest's Christ-centred pastoral love of the Church finds its most complete expression and 'supreme nourishment' in the Eucharist. Since it 'makes once again present' the Sacrifice of the Cross, Christ's complete and loving gift of Himself to the Church, His Bride, 'the priest's pastoral charity not only flows from the Eucharist but finds in the Eucharist its highest realization, just as it is from the Eucharist that he receives the grace and obligation to give his whole life a "sacrificial" dimension'.[69]

This is the context of the Holy Father's unfolding of the 'theological motivation of the Church's law on celibacy'. There is an intimate link between celibacy and sacred ordination, 'which configures the priest to Jesus Christ, the Head and Spouse of Jesus Christ':

> The Church, as the Spouse of Jesus Christ, wishes to be loved by the priest in the total and exclusive manner in which Jesus Christ her Head and Spouse loved her. Priestly celibacy, then, is the gift of self in and with Christ to His Church and expresses the priest's service to the Church in and with the Lord.[70]

The priest's celibacy is iconic and quasi-sacramental. As an icon of the Priest–Bridegroom, the priest is called to love the Church with an undivided heart reflecting something of Christ's devotion to His Bride. He should therefore be celibate.

[67] Cf. PDV 23.
[68] Ibid., 23.
[69] Ibid.
[70] Ibid., 29.

Bishops enjoy the fullness of the high priesthood and are therefore icons of the Bridegroom in a pre-eminent way (which is why they wear wedding-rings). In both East and West, they are always celibate. The bishop is the 'husband of one wife' – his particular Church (cf. 1 Tim. 3.2). St Ephrem, fourth-century Syriac Doctor of the Church, says to Bishop Abraham of Nisibis: 'Thou hast no wife, as Abraham had Sarah; behold, thy flock is thy wife. Bring up her children in thy faithfulness'.[71]

Mother of Jesus Christ and Mother of Priests

At the end of *Pastores Dabo Vobis*, as he has done in so many of the documents of his pontificate, Pope John Paul offers a prayer to Our Blessed Lady, 'Mother of Jesus Christ and Mother of Priests'.

The priest is Trinity-related, Christ-related, Church-related, and therefore also Mary-related. When the Holy Spirit configures a man to Christ the Priest in ordination, He leads him into a new intimacy of sonship with the Mother of Christ. As the Holy Father has said elsewhere, the Blessed Virgin is the supremely Christ-centred person,[72] and the surest way, for priest and seminarian and indeed every Christian, to true Christ-centredness. For this she was predestined and created, for this she was engraced from her conception; this is the office she fulfilled on earth and now continues for ever in Heaven. She has a unique place in priestly formation, for she was the first educator of the Eternal Priest, 'who became docile and subject to her motherly authority. With her example and intercession the Blessed Virgin keeps vigilant watch over the growth of vocations and priestly life in the Church'.

In the Marian prayer in *Pastores Dabo Vobis*, the Holy Father speaks in one breath of 'the priesthood of [Our Lady's] Son and sons'. Master and servants are united in one priesthood. Mary is relevant to this truth, not because she is a priest – she is not

[71] Cited in Robert Murray SJ, *Symbols of Church and Kingdom. A Study in Early Syriac Tradition* (Cambridge, 1975), p. 151.

[72] 'No one in the history of the world has been more Christocentric and Christophoric than she. And no one has been more like Him, not only with the natural likeness of mother and son, but with the likeness of the Spirit and holiness' (St Mary Major, 8/12/80). See p. 27f. above.

and could not be – but because it was by her faith and in her flesh that the eternal Son became priest. It is Mary, says Pope John Paul, who 'gave a body of flesh' to 'to the Messiah–Priest'. In her womb, in the same instant, 'through the anointing of the Holy Spirit', God the Son became man, Messiah and Priest. This is a truly wonderful fact: the Blessed Virgin Mary is the earthly origin of Christ's priesthood. Being a man, being a male, is intrinsic to his priestly office, but it was none the less in and through a woman that He took it up.

'Guard priests in your heart', prays the Pope, 'and in the Church'. Recourse to the Immaculate Heart of Mary is the most effective way of abiding safely in the Sacred Heart of Jesus and faithfully at the heart of the Church.

The second verse of the prayer takes up lofty themes from the Liturgy and the Church Fathers. It addresses Our Blessed Mother as 'Ark of the Covenant' and speaks of her accompanying the Son of man to the Temple, thereby fulfilling 'the promises given to the fathers'. The Theotokos is the consummation of the whole religious tradition of her People, truly Daughter Zion. For nine months, while she lovingly bore in her body God-made-man, she was the definitive sanctuary of the Shekinah – Ark, Temple, Tabernacle. Within His Mother's womb, Israel's promised Messiah takes up the new and everlasting priesthood, which fulfils and surpasses all the cult and sacrifice of the Old Law.

In the third verse the Pope has before his eyes the icon of Pentecost: Mary is seen as the intercessory centre of the Church, 'Mother of the Church' and 'Queen of the Apostles', praying 'to the Spirit for the new People and their Shepherds'. In the fourth and final verse he contemplates the Cross, with Mary and John at its foot. In both verses, we see the Holy Father considering Our Lady's connection with the hierarchical priesthood. These words of prayer in *Pastores Dabo Vobis* may usefully be read alongside the words of teaching in *Mulieris Dignitatem*. There, explicitly quoting and developing one of the characteristic themes of Hans Urs von Balthasar, the Holy Father distinguishes, without separating, the 'Marian' and 'Apostolic–Petrine' profiles of the Church. The apostolic priesthood within the Church is male, but the Church as a whole, served by the priesthood, is feminine. The Blessed Virgin is the Church's model and Mother, but also in a true sense the Church's embodiment and personification. In her the Church existed before a single apostle had been called:

> Mary Immaculate precedes all others, including obviously Peter himself and the Apostles. This is so, not only because Peter and the Apostles, being born of the human race under the burden of sin, form part of the Church which is 'holy from out of sinners', but also because their triple function [as teachers, priests and shepherds] has no other purpose except to form the Church in line with the ideal of sanctity already programmed and prefigured in Mary. A contemporary theologian has rightly stated that Mary is 'Queen of Apostles without any pretensions to apostolic powers: she has other and greater powers'.[73]

The bishop or priest is representative or icon or instrument of Christ, but he is not Christ. The Mother of God is the type of the Church, and she *is* the Church, the Church's first and pre-eminent member. She does not belong to the hierarchy of ministry – she is laywoman, not apostle or priest – and yet, as the Holy Father says, in the 'hierarchy of holiness' she is first.[74] In a motherly way, by love and intercession, she leads her sons – first John and then all those who share in the apostolic ministry of Holy Order – in the path of sanctity, the way of Christ- and Church-centred charity.

Theological reflection on these truths about Mary, together with filial devotion to her person, is the remedy for the ills of our time. Here, in the Ever-Virgin Theotokos, is the antidote to feminism. Here, in the heart that is all Yes to God, is the cure for all rationalistic self-centring. Here in Mary, Mother but also Bride of the Lamb, priest and seminarian learn how to love the Church.

Epilogue: Aaron
I conclude with the words of one of England's greatest poets, George Herbert (1593–1633), clergyman brother of the deistic

---

[73] MD 27, fn 55, citing Balthasar.
[74] Cf. MD 27.

philosopher, Lord Herbert of Cherbury. It has particular associations for me, because it was printed in the booklet for my first celebration of the Eucharist as an Anglican minister. George Herbert's Anglican orders, like mine, were 'absolutely null and utterly void', but his understanding of priesthood was profound and truly Catholic. In his poem 'Aaron' he gives us the essential doctrine of *Pastores Dabo Vobis*.

First, he presents the ideal priest – Aaron:

> Holiness on the head,
> Light and perfections on the breast,
> Harmonious bells below, raising the dead
> To lead them unto life and rest.
> Thus are true Aarons drest.

Then he looks at his poor self. He does not measure up:

> Profaneness in my head,
> Defects and darkness in my breast,
> A noise of passions ringing me for dead
> Unto a place where is not rest.
> Poor priest thus am I drest.

But then he remembers the indelible character of his priesthood and the grace of orders, the grace of the Christ whose power is made perfect in human weakness:

> Only another head
> I have, another heart and breast,
> Another music, making live not dead,
> Without whom I could have no rest:
> In him I am well drest.

In the fourth verse we have the Christ-centredness of priesthood, even a reference to the Sacred Heart of Jesus:

> Christ is my only head,
> My alone only heart and breast,
> My only music, striking me ev'n dead;
> That to the old man I may rest,
> And be in him new drest.

We end on an up-beat. Now the priest is facing the Church, the People of God, for Aaron's whole mission is to serve them. It is for them that he is clothed in the priesthood of Christ:

So holy in my head,
Perfect and light in my dear breast,
My doctrine tun'd by Christ (who is not dead,
But lives in me while I do rest)
Come people; Aaron's drest.[75]

George Herbert's message to priests is the same as Pope John Paul's: 'The priest always, and in an unchangeable way, finds the source of his identity in Christ the Priest'. *Christ is the answer.*

[75] *George Herbert: the Country Parson, The Temple,* ed. John N. Wall (New York, Ramsey, Toronto, 1981), p. 300.

Conclusion

I must conclude with a personal testimony. The Christo-centricity of Pope John Paul II made me a Catholic. I am a direct beneficiary of his exercise of the 'mission of the Redeemer'. At the time of his election, I was an Anglican minister, a clerical don in Oxford, but already close to making a final decision to seek admission to the One Fold of the Redeemer. I had been consciously on pilgrimage towards the Catholic Church for many years. The journey's end was certain, but I was hesitant to take the final few steps. Then, on a mellow October Sunday, I watched and listened on TV to Pope John Paul II as he delivered the homily of his inaugural Mass. 'Open the door for Christ!', he said, using words which were to become the refrain of his pontificate. I felt personally addressed. Peter was speaking through John Paul. Christ was calling me through Peter. Within a year my wife and I had been received into full communion with the Catholic Church.

Not every Roman Catholic will feel my special personal gratitude – as, so to speak, 'one of his converts' – towards the present Holy Father. But all Catholics, for the love of Christ, owe him a fidelity that engages their whole being, their every thought and action. I stress 'for the love of Christ'. 'If a man loves me', says Jesus, 'he will keep my word' (John 14.23). Now the word of Jesus to Peter is: 'Feed my lambs, tend my sheep, feed my sheep' (cf. John 21.15ff.). To love and serve Christ means to let oneself be fed and tended by Peter, not just on those rare occasions when he musters his full authority and teaches *ex cathedra*, but also, indeed especially, when day by day, in season and out, he nourishes the flock with sure and authoritative teaching. *Obsequium religiosum* and *obsequium fidei* are not to be confused, but neither should they be separated for our readiness to walk daily with Peter is the test of our openness to Jesus. The choice is stark: the Christocentricity of Catholic fidelity or the practical egocentricity of dissent:

> Why, then, do I remain in the Church? Because it is the only chance to escape from oneself, from this curse of one's importance, of one's own gravity, from the role which is identified with my own person, so that if I lost my role I would end up by falling in love with my person; to escape from all this without becoming estranged from man, because God has become man, not in a vacuum but in the community of the Church.[1]

[1] Hans Urs von Balthasar, *Elucidations*, ET (London, 1975), p. 215.

Index

Adam 23, 35, 45f., 59, 65, 75, 79, 91
Admirable Commercium 47f.
Ambrose, St xxviii
Anglicanism 109, 133
Anima ecclesiastica 65
Andrew, St xi
Assumption of Our Lady 35
Athanasius, St 57
Augustine, St xvii, 23, 36, 87, 99,
   116

Balthasar, Hans Urs von xvi, xviii,
   xx, 2, 9f., 11f., 14, 18, 21f., 29, 32,
   42f., 47f., 51, 56, 61f., 64f., 79f.,
   83ff., 86, 98, 100, 107f., 111, 124,
   129, 134
Baptism xiv, 64, 108
Beatitudes 93
Belloc, Hilaire 33
Bernard of Clairvaux, St 41
Bérulle, Pierre Cardinal de 7f.
Body, Theology of the 79f.
Boff, Leonardo 108
Bonaventure, St 3f., 7, 47, 55, 60,
   122
Bouyer, Louis 61
Buddhism 110
Bultmann, Rudolf 18, 52

Caesaropapism xx
Caffara, Carlo 100
Cappadocian Fathers 57
Capua, Council of 32
Casel OSB, Odo 8

Celibacy 67, 126ff.
Cerinthus 18
Chalcedon, Council of 81f.
Chesterton, G. K. xxi, xxv, 42, 109
Church 63ff., 95f., 101, 109f., 114
Communio sanctorum 39
Congar OP, Yves 64
Constantinople III, Council of 19
Creation 55
Cyprian, St 120
Cyril of Alexandria, St 25, 29, 31,
   117

Dante 1, 7, 33
Descartes 113
Descent into Hell 51
Dionysius the Areopagite 121
Docetism xivf.
Drama 82f.

Ephesus, Council of xiv
Epiphanius, St xvi
Eucharist xiv, 26, 54, 69ff., 96, 115,
   122, 125
Eusebius of Caesarea xix

Fatherhood of God 22
Fatima 36
Freedon 93f.

Garrigou-Lagrange OP, Reginald 5
Gilson, Etienne 6
Gnosticism xiv, xvi, 84
Gregory Nazianzen, St 97, 121
Grisez, Germain 100

Henry VIII, King xxi
Herbert, George 130ff.
Hinduism 110
Holman Hunt 13
Holy Spirit, The xiii, xv, xxv, 23ff.,
    40, 46, 53, 78, 105f., 115, 117
Honorius III, Pope xi
Hopkins SJ, Gerard Manley 41
Houselander, Caryll xvii
Hypostasis 81f.

Idealism 84
Ignatius of Antioch, St xv, xviii
Ignatius Loyola, St 67
Immaculate Conception 35f.
Irenaeus, St 57, 71, 80, 86

Jasna Gora 36
John Chrysostom, St 58, 120
John of the Cross, St xvi
John Damascene, St 29, 81
John Fisher, St xxi
Joseph, St 43
Judaism 110

Kant 113
Kingdom of God 102f., 106ff.

Lateran (649), Council of 34
Law, Natural 96, 98f.
Leo XIII, Pope 99
Leo the Great, Pope St xiii, 36, 79
Léthel OCD, Fr.-M. 6f.
Lewis, C. S. 61
Liberation Theology xvi
Louis de Montfort, St 27, 29
Lourdes 36
Lubac, Henri Cardinal de xi, xvii, 2
Lublin Thomism 5, 30
Luke, St xi

Magisterium xv, xxi, 19, 67, 96
Man, Doctrine of 75ff.
Marian Year 14
Maritain, Jacques 6, 86
Martin I, Pope St xx
Mary, Blessed Virgin xiv, xxiii, 2,
    8, 12, 24, 27ff., 45, 48, 57, 67, 71,
    78, 88f., 92, 97, 99, 105, 116,
    128ff.

Mary Magdalene, St 52
Maximus the Confessor, St xxi, 21,
    56, 59, 81
Mediatrix 38f.
Mercy of God 22f., 56
Mission 101f.
Morality xvi, 91ff.

Nestorius 25
New Age xvi
Newman, John Henry Cardinal 17,
    30, 113
Nicaea II, Council of 19
Norwid, Cyprian 5
Nuptial Mystery xvi, 26, 63, 65ff.,
    125ff.

Ordination xiv, 113ff.
Original Sin xiv, xxv, 45
Orthodox Churches, Eastern 19
Orthodoxy xxv

Paschal I, Pope St xxi
Paul, St xi, 47, 51, 80, 87, 120
Paul's Outside-the-Walls, St xi
Paul VI, Pope xi, 63, 77
Pelagianism xiv, 94, 114
Penance, Sacrament of 124
Peter, St xi, xiii, xix, xxii, 13, 17ff.,
    133
Peter Chrysologus, St 33
Pius IX, Pope 109
Pius X, Pope St xxv
Pius XII, Pope 45, 119
Poland xxiv, 85
Pole, Reginald Cardinal xxif.
Priesthood 113ff.
Protestantism 19, 64

Rahner SJ, Karl 56, 106, 111
Ratzinger, Joseph Cardinal xv,
    xxii, xvii, 32, 38f.
Resurrection xiv, 19, 51f., 59, 88
Rome xi

Salvation 45ff., 109f.
Sampson of Chichester, Bishop xxi
Scheeben, M. J. 65f.
Schmitz, Kenneth 3

Schönborn OP, Christoph 108
Scola, Angelo 79
Seifert, Josef 3
Serretti, Massimo 99f.
Silouan, Staretz 123
Soloviev, Vladimir 17
Speyr, Adrienne von xxvi
Stanislaw, St xxiii
Suarez, Francisco de xvii
Suffering 85f.

Teilhard de Chardin 8
Theodore the Studite, St xxi, 81,
121
Thomas Aquinas, St xvii, 5ff., 23f.,
49f., 54, 55, 57f., 59, 60, 80, 86,
99, 115, 121ff.
Thomas More, St xxi

Trent, Council of 70
Trinity 12, 21ff., 48, 58, 60ff., 71,
77f., 81f., 94, 104ff., 114

Urban VIII, Pope 7

Valentinus 52
Vatican Council I 37
Vatican Council II xi, 1f., 28, 31, 37,
75f., 103, 108
Virginity of Our Lady xiv, 19, 32ff.

Ware, Bishop Kallistos 30
Witness xiiff.
World, Non-Conformity to
the xxiii

Zoungrana, Archbishop 2